C.P. CAVAFY

COLLECTED POEMS

Revised Edition

PRINCETON MODERN GREEK STUDIES

This series is sponsored by the Princeton University Program
in Hellenic Studies under the auspices of the
Stanley J. Seeger Hellenic Fund

C.P. CAVAFY

COLLECTED POEMS

translated by
Edmund Keeley and Philip Sherrard

edited by
George Savidis

REVISED EDITION

PRINCETON UNIVERSITY PRESS

PRINCETON, NEW JERSEY

Translation copyright © 1975, 1992 by Edmund Keeley and Philip Sherrard
Published by Princeton University Press, 41 William Street, Princeton, New Jersey 08540

All Rights Reserved

Library of Congress Cataloging-in-Publication Data

Cavafy, Constantine, 1863–1933.
[Poems. English]
Collected poems / C. P. Cavafy; translated by Edmund Keeley and Philip Sherrard; edited by George Savidis.—Rev. ed.
p. cm.—(Princeton modern Greek studies)
(Lockert library of poetry in translation)
Includes index.
ISBN 0-691-06984-0 (Cl)—ISBN 0-691-01537-6 (Pb)
1. Cavafy, Constantine, 1863–1933—Translations into English. I. Keeley, Edmund. II. Sherrard, Philip. III. Savvidēs, Geōrgios P. IV. Title. V. Series. VI. Series: Lockert library of poetry in translation
PA5610.K2A24 1992 889'.132—dc20 92-1198

The Lockert Library of Poetry in Translation is supported by a bequest from Charles Lacy Lockert (1888–1974)

This book has been composed in Linotron Times Roman

Eleventh printing, for the revised edition, 1992

Princeton University Press books are printed on acid-free paper and meet the guidelines for permanence and durability of the Committee on Production Guidelines for Book Longevity of the Council on Library Resources

Printed in the United States of America

17 19 20 18 16

(Pbk.)

Translations included in this volume have appeared, either in earlier or current versions, in The New Yorker, The New York Review of Books, Quarterly Review of Literature, The Nation, Evergreen Review, Antaeus, The Dutton Review, University, New Letters, Shenandoah, Boundary 2, The Malahat Review, The Nassau Lit, Arion's Dolphin, Granite *and* Poetry *("The Footsteps," "The Ides of March," "Theodotos"), copyright © Modern Poetry Association, 1972*

Edmund Keeley is indebted to the John Simon Guggenheim Memorial Foundation for a fellowship that assisted his work on this volume

In memory of our friend

George Seferis

who also loved Cavafy's poems

CONTENTS

"UNPUBLISHED POEMS"

TRANSLATORS' FOREWORD
TO THE REVISED EDITION

THE COLLECTION of poems translated in this volume is the same as that of the first edition: it consists of all those poems published in the Greek edition of Cavafy's poems edited by George Savidis (Athens: Ikaros, 1963), together with a selection from the volume of "Unpublished Poems," also edited by George Savidis (Athens: Ikaros, 1968) and first published in an earlier English version in the volume *C. P. Cavafy: Passions and Ancient Days* (New York: Dial Press, 1971). Our collection has continued to be determined by these sources because we feel that they still represent the best of Cavafy's work now in print. English translations of the so-called "Early Poems" and "Repudiated Poems" are currently available in other collections or in periodicals.

Our mode of rendering Cavafy has remained more or less consistent since we offered our first broad selections of his poems in 1972 and 1975, though we have tried to freshen our renderings thereafter with each new opportunity to do so (e.g., the sixth printing of the collected edition and the selection in *Voices of Modern Greece*, Princeton, 1981). This is especially true of the present revised edition, where the resetting of the entire collection permitted us to review each poem and to make whatever alterations seemed appropriate. As in the past we have continued to strive for an equivalent discipline rather than strain to rhyme those poems—mostly early—that are strictly rhymed in the Greek; but in this latest revision we have been especially sensitive to Cavafy's other formal concerns, for example his subtle use of enjambment and his mode of establishing rhythm and emphasis through repetition. We have also chosen to render with repetitive consistency those words that Cavafy repeated often in establishing his particular personal landscape (for example, the word "idoni," which we have usually translated as "sensual pleasure"). Along with a renewed sense of responsibility toward the finer nuances and occasional eccentricities of the Greek original, we have made every effort to exercise our responsibility toward the language of poetry in English, with the hope that our renderings will live comfortably and naturally in the Anglo-American tradition.

So much critical and scholarly exploration of Cavafy's work has taken place since the first edition of this collection in 1975 that it no longer strikes us as practicable or apt to include a "Bibliographical Note" in this revised edition. We have retained, however, the "Biographical Note" essentially as it appeared originally. For this edition our editor, George Savidis, has generously revised and amplified his notes to the poems in keeping with his latest edition of the Greek text of Cavafy.

E.K.

P.S.

Katounia, Limni, Evia, 1991

"PUBLISHED POEMS"
1896-1932

WALLS

With no consideration, no pity, no shame,
they have built walls around me, thick and high.
And now I sit here feeling hopeless.
I can't think of anything else: this fate gnaws my mind—
because I had so much to do outside.
When they were building the walls, how could I not have
    noticed!
But I never heard the builders, not a sound.
Imperceptibly they have closed me off from the outside
    world.

AN OLD MAN

At the noisy end of the café, head bent
over the table, an old man sits alone,
a newspaper in front of him.

And in the miserable banality of old age
he thinks how little he enjoyed the years
when he had strength, eloquence, and looks.

He knows he's aged a lot: he sees it, feels it.
Yet it seems he was young just yesterday.
So brief an interval, so very brief.

And he thinks of Prudence, how it fooled him,
how he always believed—what madness—
that cheat who said: "Tomorrow. You have plenty of time."

He remembers impulses bridled, the joy
he sacrificed. Every chance he lost
now mocks his senseless caution.

But so much thinking, so much remembering
makes the old man dizzy. He falls asleep,
his head resting on the café table.

THE HORSES OF ACHILLES

When they saw Patroklos dead
—so brave and strong, so young—
the horses of Achilles began to weep;
their immortal nature was upset deeply
by this work of death they had to look at.
They reared their heads, tossed their long manes,
beat the ground with their hooves, and mourned
Patroklos, seeing him lifeless, destroyed,
now mere flesh only, his spirit gone,
defenseless, without breath,
turned back from life to the great Nothingness.

Zeus saw the tears of those immortal horses and felt sorry.
"At the wedding of Peleus," he said,
"I should not have acted so thoughtlessly."
Better if we hadn't given you as a gift,
my unhappy horses. What business did you have down there,
among pathetic human beings, the toys of fate.
You are free of death, you will not get old,
yet ephemeral disasters torment you.
Men have caught you up in their misery."
But it was for the eternal disaster of death
that those two gallant horses shed their tears.

PRAYER

The sea engulfed a sailor in its depths.
Unaware, his mother goes and lights
a tall candle before the ikon of our Lady,
praying for him to come back quickly, for the weather to be
    good—
her ear cocked always to the wind.
While she prays and supplicates,
the ikon listens, solemn, sad,
knowing the son she waits for never will come back.

THE FUNERAL OF SARPEDON

Zeus mourns deeply:
Patroklos has killed Sarpedon.
Now Patroklos and the Achaians rush forward
to snatch up the body, to dishonor it.

But Zeus does not tolerate that at all.
Though he let his favorite child be killed—
this the Law required—
he will at least honor him after death.
So he now sends Apollo down to the plain
with instructions about how the body should be tended.

Apollo reverently raises the hero's body
and carries it in sorrow to the river.
He washes the dust and blood away,
heals its terrible wounds so no trace is left,
pours perfume of ambrosia over it,
and dresses it in radiant Olympian robes.
He bleaches the skin, and with a pearl comb
combs out the jet black hair.
He spreads and arranges the beautiful limbs.

Now he looks like a young king, a royal charioteer—
twenty-five or twenty-six years old—
resting himself after winning
the prize in a famous race,
his chariot all gold and his horses the fastest.

Having finished his task this way,
Apollo calls for the two brothers,
Sleep and Death, and orders them
to take the body to Lykia, the rich country.

So the two brothers, Sleep and Death,
set off on foot toward the rich country, Lykia;
and when they reached the door
of the king's palace,
they handed over the honored body
and then returned to their other labors and concerns.

And once the body was received in the palace
the sad burial began, with processions and honors and dirges,
with many libations from sacred vessels,
with all pomp and circumstance.
Then skilled workers from the city
and celebrated craftsmen in stone
came to make the tombstone and the tomb.

CANDLES

Days to come stand in front of us
like a row of lighted candles—
golden, warm, and vivid candles.

Days gone by fall behind us,
a gloomy line of snuffed-out candles;
the nearest are smoking still,
cold, melted, and bent.

I don't want to look at them: their shape saddens me,
and it saddens me to remember their original light.
I look ahead at my lighted candles.

I don't want to turn for fear of seeing, terrified,
how quickly that dark line gets longer,
how quickly the snuffed-out candles proliferate.

THE FIRST STEP

The young poet Evmenis
complained one day to Theocritos:
"I have been writing for two years now
and I have composed just one idyll.
It's my only completed work.
I see, sadly, that the ladder of Poetry
is tall, extremely tall;
and from this first step I now stand on
I will never climb any higher."
Theocritos replied: "Words like that
are improper, blasphemous.
Just to be on the first step
should make you happy and proud.
To have come this far is no small achievement:
what you have done is a glorious thing.
Even this first step
is a long way above the ordinary world.
To stand on this step
you must be in your own right
a member of the city of ideas.
And it is a hard, unusual thing
to be enrolled as a citizen of that city.
Its councils are full of Legislators
no charlatan can fool.
To have come this far is no small achievement:
what you have done already is a glorious thing."

THE SOULS OF OLD MEN

Inside their worn, tattered bodies
dwell the souls of old men.
How unhappy the poor things are
and how bored by the pathetic life they live.
How they tremble for fear of losing that life, and how much
they love it, those befuddled and contradictory souls,
sitting—half comic and half tragic—
inside their old, threadbare skins.

CHE FECE . . . IL GRAN RIFIUTO

For some people the day comes
when they have to declare the great Yes
or the great No. It's clear at once who has the Yes
ready within him; and saying it,

he goes forward in honor and self-assurance.
He who refuses does not repent. Asked again,
he would still say no. Yet that no—the right no—
undermines him all his life.

INTERRUPTION

Hasty and awkward creatures of the moment,
it is we who interrupt the action of the gods.
In the palaces of Eleusis and Phthia
Demeter and Thetis initiate rituals
over high flames and heavy smoke.
But Metaneira always bursts in
from the royal quarters, hair loose, terrified,
and Peleus, scared, always intervenes.

THE WINDOWS

In these dark rooms where I live out
empty days, I circle back and forth
trying to find the windows.
It will be a great relief when a window opens.
But the windows are not there to be found—
or at least I cannot find them. And perhaps
it is better that I don't find them.
Perhaps the light will prove another tyranny.
Who knows what new things it will expose?

THERMOPYLAE

Honor to those who in the life they lead
define and guard a Thermopylae.
Never betraying what is right,
consistent and just in all they do
but showing pity also, and compassion;
generous when they are rich, and when they are poor,
still generous in small ways,
still helping as much as they can;
always speaking the truth,
yet without hating those who lie.

And even more honor is due to them
when they foresee (as many do foresee)
that in the end Ephialtis will make his appearance,
that the Medes will break through after all.

UNFAITHFULNESS

*"So although we approve of many things in Homer, this we will
not approve of . . . nor will we approve of Aeschylus when he
makes Thetis say that Apollo sang at her wedding in
celebration of her child:*

 that he would not know sickness, would live long,
 and that every blessing would be his;
 and he sang such praises that he rejoiced my heart.
 And I had hopes that the divine lips of Apollo,
 fluent with the art of prophecy, would not prove false.
 But he who proclaimed these things . . .
       he it is

who killed my son . . ."

          Plato, *Republic*, II. 383

At the marriage of Thetis and Peleus
Apollo stood up during the sumptuous wedding feast
and blessed the bridal pair
for the son who would come from their union.
"Sickness will never visit him," he said,
"and his life will be a long one."
This pleased Thetis immensely:
the words of Apollo, expert in prophecies,
seemed to guarantee the security of her child.
And when Achilles grew up
and his beauty was the boast of Thessaly,
Thetis remembered the god's words.
But one day elders arrived with the news
that Achilles had been killed at Troy.
Thetis tore her purple robes,
pulled off her rings, her bracelets,
and flung them to the ground.
And in her grief, recalling that wedding scene,
she asked what the wise Apollo was up to,
where was this poet who holds forth

so eloquently at banquets, where was this prophet
when they killed her son in his prime.
And the elders answered that Apollo himself
had gone down to Troy
and together with the Trojans had killed her son.

WAITING FOR THE BARBARIANS

What are we waiting for, assembled in the forum?

    The barbarians are due here today.

Why isn't anything happening in the senate?
Why do the senators sit there without legislating?

    Because the barbarians are coming today.
    What laws can the senators make now?
    Once the barbarians are here, they'll do the legislating.

Why did our emperor get up so early,
and why is he sitting at the city's main gate
on his throne, in state, wearing the crown?

    Because the barbarians are coming today
    and the emperor is waiting to receive their leader.
    He has even prepared a scroll to give him,
    replete with titles, with imposing names.

Why have our two consuls and praetors come out today
wearing their embroidered, their scarlet togas?
Why have they put on bracelets with so many amethysts,
and rings sparkling with magnificent emeralds?
Why are they carrying elegant canes
beautifully worked in silver and gold?

    Because the barbarians are coming today
    and things like that dazzle the barbarians.

Why don't our distinguished orators come forward as usual
to make their speeches, say what they have to say?

    Because the barbarians are coming today
    and they're bored by rhetoric and public speaking.

Why this sudden restlessness, this confusion?
(How serious people's faces have become.)
Why are the streets and squares emptying so rapidly,
everyone going home so lost in thought?

    Because night has fallen and the barbarians have not come.
    And some who have just returned from the border say
    there are no barbarians any longer.

And now, what's going to happen to us without barbarians?
They were, those people, a kind of solution.

VOICES

Voices, loved and idealized,
of those who have died, or of those
lost for us like the dead.

Sometimes they speak to us in dreams;
sometimes deep in thought the mind hears them.

And with their sound for a moment return
sounds from our life's first poetry—
like music at night, distant, fading away.

LONGINGS

Like the beautiful bodies of those who died before they had
    aged,
sadly shut away in a sumptuous mausoleum,
roses by the head, jasmine at the feet—
so appear the longings that have passed
without being satisfied, not one of them granted
a night of sensual pleasure, or one of its radiant mornings.

TROJANS

Our efforts are those of men prone to disaster;
our efforts are like those of the Trojans.
We just begin to get somewhere,
gain a little confidence,
grow almost bold and hopeful,

when something always comes up to stop us:
Achilles leaps out of the trench in front of us
and terrifies us with his violent shouting.

Our efforts are like those of the Trojans.
We think we'll change our luck
by being resolute and daring,
so we move outside ready to fight.

But when the great crisis comes,
our boldness and resolution vanish;
our spirit falters, paralyzed,
and we scurry around the walls
trying to save ourselves by running away.

Yet we're sure to fail. Up there,
high on the walls, the dirge has already begun.
They're mourning the memory, the aura of our days.
Priam and Hecuba mourn for us bitterly.

KING DIMITRIOS

*Not like a king but an actor he put
on a gray cloak instead of his royal
one and secretly went away.*

Plutarch, *Life of Dimitrios*

When the Macedonians deserted him
and showed they preferred Pyrrhos,
King Dimitrios (a noble soul) didn't behave
—so they said—
at all like a king.
He took off his golden robes,
threw away his purple buskins,
and quickly dressing himself
in simple clothes, he slipped out—
just like an actor who,
the play over,
changes his costume and goes away.

THE RETINUE OF DIONYSOS

Damon the craftsman (none better
in the Peloponnese) is giving the last touches
to his Retinue of Dionysos
carved in Parian marble: the god leading
in divine glory, with power in his stride;
after him, Intemperance; and beside Intemperance,
Intoxication pours out the satyrs' wine
from an amphora wreathed in ivy;
near them, Sweetwine, the delicate,
eyes half-closed, soporific;
and behind come the singers
Tunemaker and Melody and Reveller—
the last holding the honored processional torch
which he never lets die—and then Ceremony, so modest.
Damon carves all these. And as he works
his thoughts turn now and then
to the fee he's going to receive
from the king of Syracuse:
three talents, a large sum.
Adding this to what he has already,
he'll live grandly from now on, like a rich man,
and—think of it—he'll be able to go into politics:
he too in the Senate, he too in the Agora.

MONOTONY

One monotonous day follows another
equally monotonous. The same things
will happen again, and then will happen again,
the same moments will come and go.

A month passes by and brings another month.
Easy to guess what lies ahead:
all of yesterday's boredom.
And tomorrow ends up no longer like tomorrow.

THE FOOTSTEPS

Eagles of coral
adorn the ebony bed
where Nero lies fast asleep—
callous, peaceful, happy,
in the prime of his body's strength,
in the fine vigor of youth.

But in the alabaster hall that holds
the ancient shrine of the Aenobarbi
how restless the household gods—
they tremble, the little Lares,
and try to hide their insignificant bodies.
They've heard a terrible sound,
a deadly sound coming up the stairs,
iron footsteps that shake the staircase;
and now faint with fear, the miserable Lares
scramble to the back of the shrine,
shoving each other and stumbling,
one little god falling over another,
because they know what kind of sound that is,
know by now the footsteps of the Furies.

THAT'S THE MAN

Unknown—a stranger in Antioch—the man from Edessa
writes and writes. And at last, there,
the final canto's done. That makes

eighty-three poems in all. But so much writing,
so much versifying, the intense strain
of phrasing in Greek, has worn the poet out,
and now everything weighs down on him.

But a thought suddenly brings him out of his dejection:
the sublime "That's the man"
which Lucian once heard in his sleep.

THE CITY

You said: "I'll go to another country, go to another shore,
find another city better than this one.
Whatever I try to do is fated to turn out wrong
and my heart lies buried as though it were something dead.
How long can I let my mind moulder in this place?
Wherever I turn, wherever I happen to look,
I see the black ruins of my life, here,
where I've spent so many years, wasted them, destroyed
    them totally."

You won't find a new country, won't find another shore.
This city will always pursue you. You will walk
the same streets, grow old in the same neighborhoods,
will turn gray in these same houses.
You will always end up in this city. Don't hope for things
    elsewhere:
there is no ship for you, there is no road.
As you've wasted your life here, in this small corner,
you've destroyed it everywhere else in the world.

THE SATRAPY

Too bad that, cut out as you are
for grand and noble acts,
this unfair fate of yours
never offers encouragement, always denies you success;
that cheap habits get in your way,
pettiness, or indifference.
And how terrible the day you give in
(the day you let go and give in)
and take the road for Susa
and go to King Artaxerxes,
who, well-disposed, gives you a place at his court
and offers you satrapies and things like that—
things you don't want at all,
though, in despair, you accept them just the same.
You long for something else, ache for other things:
praise from the Demos and the Sophists,
that hard-won, that priceless acclaim—
the Agora, the Theatre, the Crowns of Laurel.
You can't get any of these from Artaxerxes,
you'll never find any of these in the satrapy,
and without them, what kind of life will you live?

THE IDES OF MARCH

Guard, O my soul, against pomp and glory.
And if you cannot curb your ambitions,
at least pursue them hesitantly, cautiously.
And the higher you go,
the more searching and careful you need to be.

And when you reach your summit, Caesar at last—
when you assume the role of someone that famous—
then be especially careful as you go out into the street,
a conspicuous man of power with your retinue;
and should a certain Artemidoros
come up to you out of the crowd, bringing a letter,
and say hurriedly: "Read this at once.
There are things in it important for you to see,"
be sure to stop; be sure to postpone
all talk or business; be sure to brush off
all those who salute and bow to you
(they can be seen later); let even
the Senate itself wait—and find out immediately
what grave message Artemidoros has for you.

THINGS ENDED

Possessed by fear and suspicion,
mind agitated, eyes alarmed,
we desperately invent ways out,
plan how to avoid the inevitable
danger that threatens us so terribly.
Yet we're mistaken, that's not the danger ahead:
the information was false
(or we didn't hear it, or didn't get it right).
Another disaster, one we never imagined,
suddenly, violently, descends upon us,
and finding us unprepared—there's no time left—
sweeps us away.

SCULPTOR OF TYANA

As you'll have heard, I'm no beginner.
I've handled a lot of stone in my time,
and in my own country, Tyana, I'm pretty well known.
Actually, senators here have also commissioned
a number of statues from me.

                              Let me show you
a few of them. Notice this Rhea:
reverential, all fortitude, very old.
Notice Pompey. And Marius here,
and Paulus Aemilius, and Scipio Africanus.
The likeness as close as I could make it.
And Patroklos (I still have to touch him up a bit).
Near those pieces of yellowish marble there
stands Kaisarion.

And for some time now I've been busy
working on a Poseidon. I'm studying
his horses in particular: how to shape them exactly.
They have to be made so light
that it's clear their bodies, their legs,
are not touching the earth but galloping over water.

But here's my favorite work,
wrought with the utmost care and feeling.
This one—it was a summer day, very hot,
and my mind rose to ideal things—
this one came to me in a vision, this young Hermes.

THE GOD ABANDONS ANTONY

When suddenly, at midnight, you hear
an invisible procession going by
with exquisite music, voices,
don't mourn your luck that's failing now,
work gone wrong, your plans
all proving deceptive—don't mourn them uselessly.
As one long prepared, and graced with courage,
say goodbye to her, the Alexandria that is leaving.
Above all, don't fool yourself, don't say
it was a dream, your ears deceived you:
don't degrade yourself with empty hopes like these.
As one long prepared, and graced with courage,
as is right for you who were given this kind of city,
go firmly to the window
and listen with deep emotion, but not
with the whining, the pleas of a coward;
listen—your final delectation—to the voices,
to the exquisite music of that strange procession,
and say goodbye to her, to the Alexandria you are losing.

IONIC

That we've broken their statues,
that we've driven them out of their temples,
doesn't mean at all that the gods are dead.
O land of Ionia, they're still in love with you,
their souls still keep your memory.
When an August dawn wakes over you,
your atmosphere is potent with their life,
and sometimes a young ethereal figure,
indistinct, in rapid flight,
wings across your hills.

THE GLORY OF THE PTOLEMIES

I'm Lagides, king, absolute master
(through my power and wealth) of sensual pleasure.
There's no Macedonian, no barbarian, equal to me
or even approaching me. The son of Selefkos
is really a joke with his cheap lechery.
But if you're looking for other things, note this too:
my city's the greatest preceptor, queen of the Greek world,
genius of all knowledge, of every art.

ITHAKA

As you set out for Ithaka
hope the voyage is a long one,
full of adventure, full of discovery.
Laistrygonians and Cyclops,
angry Poseidon—don't be afraid of them:
you'll never find things like that on your way
as long as you keep your thoughts raised high,
as long as a rare excitement
stirs your spirit and your body.
Laistrygonians and Cyclops,
wild Poseidon—you won't encounter them
unless you bring them along inside your soul,
unless your soul sets them up in front of you.

Hope the voyage is a long one.
May there be many a summer morning when,
with what pleasure, what joy,
you come into harbors seen for the first time;
may you stop at Phoenician trading stations
to buy fine things,
mother of pearl and coral, amber and ebony,
sensual perfume of every kind—
as many sensual perfumes as you can;
and may you visit many Egyptian cities
to gather stores of knowledge from their scholars.

Keep Ithaka always in your mind.
Arriving there is what you are destined for.
But do not hurry the journey at all.
Better if it lasts for years,
so you are old by the time you reach the island,

wealthy with all you have gained on the way,
not expecting Ithaka to make you rich.

Ithaka gave you the marvelous journey.
Without her you would not have set out.
She has nothing left to give you now.

And if you find her poor, Ithaka won't have fooled you.
Wise as you will have become, so full of experience,
you will have understood by then what these Ithakas mean.

DANGEROUS THOUGHTS

Said Myrtias (a Syrian student
in Alexandria during the reign
of the Emperor Konstans and the Emperor Konstantios;
in part a heathen, in part christianized):
"Strengthened by study and reflection.
I won't fear my passions like a coward;
I'll give my body to sensual pleasures,
to enjoyments I've dreamed of,
to the most audacious erotic desires,
to the lascivious impulses of my blood,
with no fear at all, because when I wish—
and I'll have the will-power, strengthened
as I shall be by study and reflection—
when I wish, at critical moments I will recover
my spirit, ascetic as it was before."

PHILHELLENE

Make sure the engraving is done skillfully.
The expression serious, majestic.
The diadem preferably somewhat narrow:
I don't like that broad kind the Parthians wear.
The inscription, as usual, in Greek:
nothing excessive, nothing pompous—
we don't want the proconsul to take it the wrong way:
he's always nosing things out and reporting back to Rome—
but of course giving me due honor.
Something very special on the other side:
some discus-thrower, young, good-looking.
Above all I urge you to see to it
(Sithaspis, for God's sake don't let them forget)
that after "King" and "Savior,"
they engrave "Philhellene" in elegant characters.
Now don't try to be clever
with your "where are the Greeks?" and "what things Greek
here behind Zagros, out beyond Phraata?"
Since so many others more barbarian than ourselves
choose to inscribe it, we will inscribe it too.
And besides, don't forget that sometimes
sophists do come to us from Syria,
and versifiers, and other triflers of that kind.
So we are not, I think, un-Greek.

HERODIS ATTIKOS

What glory, this, for Herodis Attikos!

Alexander of Selefkia, one of our good sophists,
on reaching Athens to lecture
finds the city deserted because Herodis
was in the countryside. And all the young men
had followed him there to hear him.
This makes sophist Alexander
write Herodis a letter
begging him to send the Greeks back.
And the tactful Herodis answers at once:
"Along with the Greeks, I'm coming too."

How many young men now in Alexandria,
in Antioch or in Beirut
(being trained by Hellenism as its future orators),
meeting at their choice banquets
where the talk is sometimes about fine sophistry,
sometimes about their exquisite love affairs,
are suddenly distracted and fall silent.
Their glasses untouched in front of them,
they think about Herodis' good fortune—
what other sophist has been given this kind of honor?
Whatever his wish, whatever he does,
the Greeks (the Greeks!) follow him,
not to criticize or debate,
not even to choose any longer,
only to follow.

ALEXANDRIAN KINGS

The Alexandrians turned out in force
to see Cleopatra's children,
Kaisarion and his little brothers,
Alexander and Ptolemy, who for the first time
had been taken out to the Gymnasium,
to be proclaimed kings there
before a brilliant array of soldiers.

Alexander: they declared him
king of Armenia, Media, and the Parthians.
Ptolemy: they declared him
king of Cilicia, Syria, and Phoenicia.
Kaisarion was standing in front of the others,
dressed in pink silk,
on his chest a bunch of hyacinths,
his belt a double row of amethysts and sapphires,
his shoes tied with white ribbons
prinked with rose-colored pearls.
They declared him greater than his little brothers,
they declared him King of Kings.

The Alexandrians knew of course
that this was all mere words, all theatre.

But the day was warm and poetic,
the sky a pale blue,
the Alexandrian Gymnasium
a complete artistic triumph,
the courtiers wonderfully sumptuous,
Kaisarion all grace and beauty
(Cleopatra's son, blood of the Lagids);

and the Alexandrians thronged to the festival
full of enthusiasm, and shouted acclamations
in Greek, and Egyptian, and some in Hebrew,
charmed by the lovely spectacle—
though they knew of course what all this was worth,
what empty words they really were, these kingships.

COME BACK

Come back often and take hold of me,
sensation that I love come back and take hold of me—
when the body's memory awakens
and an old longing again moves into the blood,
when lips and skin remember
and hands feel as though they touch again.

Come back often, take hold of me in the night
when lips and skin remember . . .

IN CHURCH

I love the church: its labara,
its silver vessels, its candleholders,
the lights, the ikons, the pulpit.

Whenever I go there, into a church of the Greeks,
with its aroma of incense,
its liturgical chanting and harmony,
the majestic presence of the priests,
dazzling in their ornate vestments,
the solemn rhythm of their gestures—
my thoughts turn to the great glories of our race,
to the splendor of our Byzantine heritage.

VERY SELDOM

He's an old man. Used up and bent,
crippled by time and indulgence,
he slowly walks along the narrow street.
But when he goes inside his house to hide
the shambles of his old age, his mind turns
to the share in youth that still belongs to him.

His verse is now recited by young men.
His visions come before their lively eyes.
Their healthy sensual minds,
their shapely taut bodies
stir to his perception of the beautiful.

AS MUCH AS YOU CAN

And if you can't shape your life the way you want,
at least try as much as you can
not to degrade it
by too much contact with the world,
by too much activity and talk.

Try not to degrade it by dragging it along,
taking it around and exposing it so often
to the daily silliness
of social events and parties,
until it comes to seem a boring hanger-on.

FOR THE SHOP

He wrapped them up carefully, neatly,
in expensive green silk.
Roses of rubies, lilies of pearl
violets of amethyst: beautiful according to his taste,
to his desire, his vision—not as he saw them in nature
or studied them. He'll leave them in the safe,
examples of his bold, his skillful work.
Whenever a customer comes into the shop,
he brings out other things to sell—first class ornaments:
bracelets, chains, necklaces, rings.

I WENT

I didn't hold myself back. I gave in completely and went,
went to those delectations that were half real,
half wrought by my own mind,
went into the brilliant night
and drank strong wine,
the way the champions of pleasure drink.

TOMB OF THE GRAMMARIAN LYSIAS

In the Beirut library, just to the right as you go in,
we buried wise Lysias, the grammarian.
The spot is beautifully chosen.
We put him near those things of his
that he remembers maybe even there:
comments, texts, grammars, variants,
voluminous studies of Greek idioms.
Also, this way, as we go to the books,
we'll see, we'll honor his tomb.

TOMB OF EVRION

In this tomb—ornately designed,
the whole of syenite stone,
covered by so many violets, so many lilies—
lies handsome Evrion,
an Alexandrian, twenty-five years old.
On his father's side, he was of old Macedonian stock,
on his mother's side, descended from a line of magistrates.
He studied philosophy with Aristokleitos,
rhetoric with Paros, and at Thebes
the sacred scriptures. He wrote a history
of the province of Arsinoites. That at least will survive.
But we've lost what was really precious: his form—
like a vision of Apollo.

CHANDELIER

In a room—empty, small, four walls only,
covered with green cloth—
a beautiful chandelier burns, all fire;
and in each of its flames a sensual fever,
a lascivious urge, glows with heat.

In the small room, radiantly lit
by the chandelier's hot fire,
no ordinary light breaks out.
Not for timid bodies
the rapture of this heat.

LONG AGO

I'd like to speak of this memory . . .
but it's so faded now . . . as though nothing is left—
because it was so long ago, in my early adolescent years.

A skin as though of jasmine . . .
that August evening—was it August?—
I can still just recall the eyes: blue, I think they were . . .
Ah yes, blue: a sapphire blue.

BUT THE WISE PERCEIVE THINGS ABOUT TO HAPPEN

> *"For the gods perceive future things,*
> *ordinary people things in the present, but*
> *the wise perceive things about to happen."*
>
> Philostratos, *Life of Apollonios of*
> *Tyana*, viii, 7.

Ordinary people know what's happening now,
the gods know future things
because they alone are totally enlightened.
Of what's to come the wise perceive
things about to happen.

Sometimes during moments of intense study
their hearing's troubled: the hidden sound
of things approaching reaches them,
and they listen reverently, while in the street outside
the people hear nothing whatsoever.

THEODOTOS

If you are one of the truly elect,
be careful how you attain your eminence.
However much you are acclaimed, however much
the cities praise the great things you have done
in Italy and Thessaly,
whatever honors
your admirers decree for you in Rome,
your elation, your triumph will not last,
nor will you feel yourself superior—superior indeed!—
when Theodotos brings you, in Alexandria,
on a blood-stained tray,
miserable Pompey's head.

And do not be too sure that in your life—
restricted, regulated, prosaic—
spectacular and horrible things like that do not happen.
Maybe this very moment Theodotos—
bodiless, invisible—
enters some neighbor's tidy house
carrying an equally repulsive head.

AT THE CAFÉ DOOR

Something they said beside me
made me look toward the café door,
and I saw that lovely body which seemed
as though Eros in his mastery had fashioned it,
joyfully shaping its well-formed limbs,
molding its tall build,
shaping its face tenderly,
and leaving, with a touch of the fingers,
a particular nuance on the brow, the eyes, the lips.

HE SWEARS

He swears every now and then to begin a better life.
But when night comes with its own counsel,
its own compromises and prospects—
when night comes with its own power
of a body that needs and demands,
he goes back, lost, to the same fatal pleasure.

ONE NIGHT

The room was cheap and sordid,
hidden above the suspect taverna.
From the window you could see the alley,
dirty and narrow. From below
came the voices of workmen
playing cards, enjoying themselves.

And there on that common, humble bed
I had love's body, had those intoxicating lips,
red and sensual,
red lips of such intoxication
that now as I write, after so many years,
in my lonely house, I'm drunk with passion again.

MORNING SEA

Let me stop here. Let me, too, look at nature awhile.
The brilliant blue of the morning sea, of the cloudless sky,
the yellow shore; all lovely,
all bathed in light.

Let me stand here. And let me pretend I see all this
(I really did see it for a minute when I first stopped)
and not my usual day-dreams here too,
my memories, those images of sensual pleasure.

PICTURED

My work, I'm very careful about it, and I love it.
But today I'm discouraged by how slowly it's going.
The day has affected my mood.
It gets darker and darker. Endless wind and rain.
I'm more in the mood for looking than for writing.
In this picture, I'm now gazing at a handsome boy
who is lying down close to a spring,
exhausted from running.
What a handsome boy; what a heavenly noon
has caught him up in sleep.
I sit and gaze like this for a long time,
recovering through art from the effort of creating it.

OROPHERNIS

The figure on this four drachma coin
who seems to have a smile on his face—
his beautiful, delicate face—
this is Orophernis, son of Ariarathis.

A child, they threw him out of Cappadocia,
out of his great ancestral palace,
and sent him to grow up in Ionia,
to be forgotten there among foreigners.

Oh those exquisite Ionian nights
when fearlessly, and entirely in a Greek way,
he came to know sensual pleasure totally.
In his heart, Asiatic always,
but in manners and language, a Greek;
with his turquoise jewelry, his Greek clothes,
his body perfumed with oil of jasmine,
he was the most handsome, the most perfect
of Ionia's handsome young men.

Later, when the Syrians entered Cappadocia
and made him king,
he became fully engrossed in his kingship
so as to enjoy himself in a new way each day,
greedily hoarding gold and silver,
delightedly gloating over
the piles of wealth glittering before his eyes.
As for worrying about the country and running it—
he had no idea what was going on around him.

The Cappadocians quickly got rid of him,
and he ended up in Syria, at the palace of Dimitrios,
where he spent his time amusing himself and loafing.

But one day unfamiliar thoughts
broke in on his completely idle life:
he remembered how through his mother Antiochis
and that old grandmother Stratoniki
he too was connected with the Syrian crown,
he too almost a Selefkid.
For a while he gave up lechery and drink,
and ineptly, half dazed,
tried to start an intrigue,
do something, come up with a plan;
but he failed pitifully and was reduced to nothing.

His end must have been recorded somewhere only to be lost:
or maybe history passed over it
and rightly didn't bother to notice
a thing so trivial.

The figure on this four drachma coin,
a trace of whose young charm can still be seen,
a ray of his poetic beauty—
this sensuous commemoration of an Ionian boy,
this is Orophernis, son of Ariarathis.

THE BATTLE OF MAGNESIA

He's lost his old fire, his courage.
Now his tired, almost decrepit body
will be his first concern. And the rest of his life he'll spend
without worrying. So Philip says, anyway.
Tonight he's playing a game with dice;
he's in a mood to amuse himself.
Cover the table with roses. What if Antiochos
was defeated at Magnesia? They say
the bulk of his brilliant army was totally crushed.
Maybe they're stretching it a bit; it can't all be true.
Let's hope so anyway. Because though enemies, they do
    belong to our race.
But one "let's hope so" is enough. Perhaps even too much.
Of course Philip won't put off the festivities.
However much his life has worn him out,
one blessing remains: his memory is still intact.
He recalls the extent of their mourning in Syria, the kind of
    sorrow they felt,
when Macedonia, their motherland, was smashed to pieces.
Let the banquet begin. Slaves! The music, the lights!

MANUEL KOMNINOS

One dreary September day
Emperor Manuel Komninos
felt his death was near.
The court astrologers—bribed, of course—went on babbling
about how many years he still had to live.
But while they were having their say,
he remembered an old religious custom
and ordered ecclesiastical vestments
to be brought from a monastery,
and he put them on, glad to assume
the modest image of a priest or monk.

Happy all those who believe,
and like Emperor Manuel end their lives
dressed modestly in their faith.

THE DISPLEASURE OF SELEFKIDIS

Dimitrios Selefkidis was displeased
to learn that a Ptolemy
had reached Italy in such a squalid state:
poorly dressed and on foot,
with only three or four slaves. This way
their dynasty will become a joke,
the laughter of Rome.
Selefkidis knows of course
that basically they have become something like servants
to the Romans; he also knows
that the Romans give and take away
their thrones arbitrarily, as they please.
But they should maintain a certain dignity,
at least in their appearance;
they should not forget that they are still kings,
are still (alas) called kings.

This is why Dimitrios Selefkidis was displeased;
and right away he offered Ptolemy
purple robes, a magnificent diadem,
precious jewels, numerous servants and retainers,
his most expensive horses,
so that he might present himself at Rome as he should,
as an Alexandrian Greek monarch.

But Ptolemy, who had come to beg,
knew his business and refused it all:
he didn't have the slightest need for these luxuries.
Shabbily dressed, humble, he entered Rome,

put himself up in the house of a minor artisan,
and then he presented himself
as a poor, ill-fated creature to the Senate
in order to make his begging more effective.

WHEN THEY COME ALIVE

Try to keep them, poet,
those erotic visions of yours,
however few of them there are that can be stilled.
Put them, half-hidden, in your lines.
Try to hold them, poet,
when they come alive in your mind
at night or in the brightness of noon.

IN THE STREET

His attractive face a bit pale,
his chestnut eyes looking tired, dazed,
twenty-five years old but could be taken for twenty,
with something of the artist in the way he dresses
—the color of his tie, shape of his collar—
he drifts aimlessly down the street,
as though still hypnotized by the illicit pleasure,
the very illicit pleasure that has just been his.

BEFORE THE STATUE
OF ENDYMION

I have come from Miletos to Latmos
on a white chariot drawn by four snow-white mules,
all their trappings silver.
I sailed from Alexandria in a purple trireme
to perform sacred rites—
sacrifices and libations—in honor of Endymion.
And here is the statue. I now gaze in ecstasy
at Endymion's famous beauty.
My slaves empty baskets of jasmine
and auspicious tributes revive the pleasure of ancient days.

IN A TOWN OF OSROINI

Yesterday, around midnight, they brought us our friend
 Remon,
who'd been wounded in a taverna fight.
Through the windows we left wide open,
the moon cast light over his beautiful body as he lay on the
 bed.
We're a mixture here: Syrians, migrated Greeks, Armenians,
 Medes.
Remon too is one of this kind. But last night,
when the moon shone on his sensual face,
our thoughts went back to Plato's Charmidis.

PASSING THROUGH

The things he timidly imagined as a schoolboy
are openly revealed to him now. And he wanders around,
stays out all night, gets involved. And as is right (for our kind
    of art)
his blood—fresh and hot—
is relished by sensual pleasure. His body is overcome
by forbidden erotic ecstasy; and his young limbs
give in to it completely.

                    In this way a simple boy
becomes something worth our looking at, for a moment
he too passes through the exalted World of Poetry,
the young sensualist with blood fresh and hot.

FOR AMMONIS, WHO DIED
AT 29, IN 610

Raphael, they're asking you to write a few lines
as an epitaph for the poet Ammonis:
something very tasteful and polished. You can do it,
you're the one to write something suitable
for the poet Ammonis, our Ammonis.

Of course you'll speak about his poems—
but say something too about his beauty,
about his subtle beauty that we loved.

Your Greek is always elegant and musical.
But we want all your craftsmanship now.
Our sorrow and our love move into a foreign language.
Pour your Egyptian feeling into the Greek you use.

Raphael, your verses, you know, should be written
so they contain something of our life within them,
so the rhythm, so every phrase clearly shows
that an Alexandrian is writing about an Alexandrian.

ONE OF THEIR GODS

When one of them moved through the marketplace of
    Selefkia
just as it was getting dark—
moved like a young man, tall, extremely handsome,
with the joy of being immortal in his eyes,
with his black and perfumed hair—
the people going by would gaze at him,
and one would ask the other if he knew him,
if he was a Greek from Syria, or a stranger.
But some who looked more carefully
would understand and step aside;
and as he disappeared under the arcades,
among the shadows and the evening lights,
going toward the quarter that lives
only at night, with orgies and debauchery,
with every kind of intoxication and desire,
they would wonder which of Them it could be,
and for what suspicious pleasure
he had come down into the streets of Selefkia
from the August Celestial Mansions.

IN THE EVENING

It wouldn't have lasted long anyway—
the experience of years makes that clear.
Even so, Fate did put an end to it a bit abruptly.
It was soon over, that wonderful life.
Yet how strong the scents were,
what a magnificent bed we lay in,
what pleasure we gave our bodies.

An echo from my days given to sensuality,
an echo from those days came back to me,
something of the fire of the young life we shared:
I picked up a letter again,
and I read it over and over till the light faded away.

Then, sad, I went out on to the balcony,
went out to change my thoughts at least by seeing
something of this city I love,
a little movement in the street and the shops.

TO SENSUAL PLEASURE

My life's joy and incense: recollection of those hours
when I found and captured sensual pleasure as I wanted it.
My life's joy and incense: that I refused
all indulgence in routine love affairs.

GRAY

While looking at a half-gray opal
I remembered two lovely gray eyes—
it must be twenty years ago I saw them . . .

. . . .

We were lovers for a month.
Then he went away to work, I think in Smyrna,
and we never met again.

Those gray eyes will have lost their beauty—if he's still alive;
that lovely face will have spoiled.

Memory, keep them the way they were.
And, memory, whatever of that love you can bring back,
whatever you can, bring back tonight.

TOMB OF IASIS

I, Iasis, lie here—the young man
famous for his good looks in this great city.
Men of learning admired me, so did simple, superficial
  people.
I took equal pleasure in both.

But from being considered so often a Narcissus and Hermes,
excess wore me out, killed me. Traveler,
if you're an Alexandrian, you won't blame me.
You know the pace of our life—its fever, its unsurpassable
  sensuality.

IN THE MONTH OF ATHYR

I can just read the inscription on this ancient stone.
"Lo[r]d Jesus Christ." I make out a "So[u]l."
"In the mon[th] of Athyr" "Lefkio[s] went to sleep."
Where his age is mentioned—"lived to the age of"—
the Kappa Zeta shows that he went to sleep a young man.
In the corroded part I see "Hi[m] . . . Alexandrian."
Then there are three badly mutilated lines—
though I can pick out a few words, like "our tea[r]s,"
    "grief,"
then "tears" again, and "sorrow to [us] his [f]riends."
I think Lefkios must have been greatly loved.
In the month of Athyr Lefkios went to sleep.

I'VE LOOKED SO MUCH. . . .

I've looked on beauty so much
that my vision overflows with it.

The body's lines. Red lips. Sensual limbs.
Hair as though stolen from Greek statues,
always lovely, even uncombed,
and falling slightly over pale foreheads.
Figures of love, as my poetry desired them
. . . . in the nights when I was young,
encountered secretly in those nights.

TOMB OF IGNATIOS

Here I'm not the Kleon famous in Alexandria
(where they're not easily dazzled)
for my marvelous houses, my gardens,
for my horses and chariots,
for the jewels and silks I wore.
Far from it—here I'm not that Kleon:
his twenty-eight years are to be wiped out.
I'm Ignatios, lector, who came to his senses very late;
but even so, in that way I lived ten happy months
in the peace, the security of Christ.

DAYS OF 1903

I never found them again—all lost so quickly . . .
the poetic eyes, the pale face . . .
in the darkening street . . .

I never found them again—mine entirely by chance,
and so easily given up,
then longed for so painfully.
The poetic eyes, the pale face,
those lips—I never found them again.

THE WINDOW OF THE TOBACCO SHOP

They stood among many others
close to a lighted tobacco shop window.
Their glances met by chance
and timidly, haltingly expressed
the illicit desire of their bodies.
Then a few uneasy steps along the street
until they smiled, and nodded slightly.

And after that the closed carriage,
the sensitive approach of body to body,
hands linked, lips meeting.

KAISARION

Partly to throw light on a certain period,
partly to kill an hour or two,
last night I picked up and read
a volume of inscriptions about the Ptolemies.
The lavish praise and flattery are much the same
for each of them. All are brilliant,
glorious, mighty, benevolent;
everything they undertake is full of wisdom.
As for the women of their line, the Berenices and Cleopatras,
they too, all of them, are marvelous.

When I'd verified the facts I wanted
I would have put the book away had not a brief
insignificant mention of King Kaisarion
suddenly caught my eye . . .

And there you were with your indefinable charm.
Because we know
so little about you from history,
I could fashion you more freely in my mind.
I made you good-looking and sensitive.
My art gives your face
a dreamy, an appealing beauty.
And so completely did I imagine you
that late last night,
as my lamp went out—I let it go out on purpose—
it seemed you came into my room,
it seemed you stood there in front of me, looking just as you
    would have

in conquered Alexandria,
pale and weary, ideal in your grief,
still hoping they might take pity on you,
those scum who whispered: ''Too many Caesars.''

BODY, REMEMBER. . . .

Body, remember not only how much you were loved,
not only the beds you lay on,
but also those desires that glowed openly
in eyes that looked at you,
trembled for you in the voices—
only some chance obstacle frustrated them.
Now that it's all finally in the past,
it seems almost as if you gave yourself
to those desires too—how they glowed,
remember, in eyes that looked at you,
remember, body, how they trembled for you in those voices.

TOMB OF LANIS

The Lanis you loved, Markos, isn't here
in this tomb you come to weep by, lingering hours on end.
The Lanis you loved is closer to you
when you're in your room at home and you look at his
    portrait—
the portrait that still keeps something of what was valuable in
    him,
something of what it was you used to love.

Remember, Markos, that time you brought in
the famous Kyrenian painter from the Proconsul's palace?
What artistic subtlety he used trying to persuade you both,
the minute he saw your friend,
that he absolutely must do him as Hyacinth.
In that way his portrait would come to be better known.

But your Lanis didn't hire out his beauty like that:
reacting strongly, he told him to portray
neither Hyacinth nor anyone else,
but Lanis, son of Rametichos, an Alexandrian.

UNDERSTANDING

The years of my youth, my sensual life—
how clearly I see their meaning now.

How needless the repentance, how futile . . .

But I didn't see the meaning then.

In the loose living of my early years
the impulses of my poetry were shaped,
the boundaries of my art were laid down.

That's why the repentance was so fickle.
And my resolutions to hold back, to change,
lasted two weeks at the most.

NERO'S DEADLINE

Nero wasn't worried at all when he heard
the utterance of the Delphic Oracle:
"Beware the age of seventy-three."
Plenty of time to enjoy himself still.
He's thirty. The deadline
the god has given him is quite enough
to cope with future dangers.

Now, a little tired, he'll return to Rome—
but wonderfully tired from that journey
devoted entirely to pleasure:
theatres, garden-parties, stadiums . . .
evenings in the cities of Achaia . . .
and, above all, the sensual delight of naked bodies . . .

So much for Nero. And in Spain Galba
secretly musters and drills his army—
Galba, the old man in his seventy-third year.

ENVOYS FROM ALEXANDRIA

For centuries they hadn't seen gifts at Delphi
as wonderful as those sent by the two brothers,
the rival Ptolemaic kings. But now that they have them,
the priests are nervous about the oracle. They'll need
all their experience to decide
how to express it tactfully, which of the two—
of two brothers like these—will have to be offended.
And so they meet secretly at night
to discuss the family affairs of the Lagids.

But suddenly the envoys are back. They're taking their leave.
Returning to Alexandria, they say. And they don't ask
for an oracle at all. The priests are delighted to hear it
(they're to keep the marvelous gifts, that goes without saying)
but they're also completely bewildered,
having no idea what this sudden indifference means.
They do not know that yesterday the envoys heard serious
        news:
the "oracle" was pronounced in Rome; the partition was
        decided there.

ARISTOVOULOS

The palace weeps, the king weeps,
King Herod grieves inconsolably,
the whole town weeps for Aristovoulos
drowned by accident, so wastefully,
while playing in the water with his friends.

And when the news spreads abroad,
when it reaches Syria,
even many Greeks will be sad,
poets and sculptors will mourn—
they've heard of Aristovoulos,
yet their imagination could never conceive
a young man with the beauty of this boy:
what statue of a god can Antioch boast
to compare with this child of Israel?

The First Princess, his mother, the leading Hebrew
    woman,
weeps and laments:
Alexandra weeps and laments over the tragedy.
But the minute she is alone, her lamenting disappears.
She howls, rails, swears, curses.
How they've fooled her, how they've cheated her,
how they've finally had their way,
devastating the house of the Asmonaeans!
How did he pull it off, that crook of a king,
scheming, crafty, vicious,
how did he do it? A plot so fiendish
that even Mariamme didn't sense a thing.
Had she sensed something, had she suspected,
she would have found a way of saving her brother:
she is a queen after all, she could have done something.

How those spiteful women, Kypros and Salome,
those sluts Kypros and Salome—
how they'll crow now, gloating in secret.
And to be powerless,
forced to pretend she believes their lies,
powerless to go to the people,
to go out and shout to the Hebrews,
to tell them, tell them how the murder was carried out.

IN THE HARBOR-TOWN

Emis—young, twenty-eight—
reached this Syrian harbor in a Tenian ship,
his plan to learn the incense trade.
But ill during the voyage,
he died as soon as he was put ashore.
His burial, the poorest possible, took place here.
A few hours before dying he whispered something
about "home," about "very old parents."
But nobody knew who they were,
or what country he called home
in the great panhellenic world.
Better that way; because as it is,
though he lies buried in this harbor-town,
his parents will always have the hope he's still alive.

AIMILIANOS MONAI, ALEXANDRIAN,
A.D. 628-655

Out of talk, appearance, and manners
I will make an excellent suit of armor;
and in this way I will face malicious people
without feeling the slightest fear or weakness.

They will try to injure me. But of those
who come near me none will know
where to find my wounds, my vulnerable places,
under the deceptions that will cover me.

So boasted Aimilianos Monai.
One wonders if he ever made that suit of armor.
In any case, he did not wear it long.
At the age of twenty-seven, he died in Sicily.

SINCE NINE O'CLOCK

Half past twelve. Time has gone by quickly
since nine o'clock when I lit the lamp
and sat down here. I've been sitting without reading,
without speaking. Completely alone in the house,
whom could I talk to?

Since nine o'clock when I lit the lamp
the shade of my young body
has come to haunt me, to remind me
of shut scented rooms,
of past sensual pleasure—what daring pleasure.
And it's also brought back to me
streets now unrecognizable,
bustling night clubs now closed,
theatres and cafés no longer there.

The shade of my young body
also brought back the things that make us sad:
family grief, separations,
the feelings of my own people, feelings
of the dead so little acknowledged.

Half past twelve. How the time has gone by.
Half past twelve. How the years have gone by.

OUTSIDE THE HOUSE

Walking yesterday in an outlying neighborhood,
I went by the house
I used to go to when I was very young.
There Eros with his magnificent power
had taken hold of my body.

                  And yesterday
when I walked along the old road,
the shops, the sidewalks, the stones,
walls and balconies and windows—
all were suddenly made beautiful by the spell of love:
nothing ugly was left there.

And as I stood gazing at the door,
stood there lingering outside the house,
my whole being radiated
the sensual emotion stored up inside me.

THE NEXT TABLE

He must be barely twenty-two years old—
yet I'm certain that almost that many years ago
I enjoyed the very same body.

It isn't erotic fever at all.
And I've been in the casino for a few minutes only,
so I haven't had time to drink a great deal.
I enjoyed that very same body.

And if I don't remember where, this one lapse of memory
    doesn't mean a thing.

There, now that he's sitting down at the next table,
I recognize every motion he makes—and under his clothes
I see again the limbs I loved, naked.

THE AFTERNOON SUN

This room, how well I know it.
Now they're renting it, and the one next to it,
as offices. The whole house has become
an office building for agents, merchants, companies.

This room, how familiar it is.

Here, near the door, was the couch,
a Turkish carpet in front of it.
Close by, the shelf with two yellow vases.
On the right—no, opposite—a wardrobe with a mirror.
In the middle the table where he wrote,
and the three big wicker chairs.
Beside the window was the bed
where we made love so many times.

They must still be around somewhere, those old things.

Beside the window was the bed;
the afternoon sun fell across half of it.

. . . One afternoon at four o'clock we separated
for a week only . . . And then—
that week became forever.

COMES TO REST

It must have been one o'clock at night
or half past one.

               A corner in the wine-shop
behind the wooden partition:
except for the two of us the place completely empty.
An oil lamp barely gave it light.
The waiter, on duty all day, was sleeping by the door.

No one could see us. But anyway,
we were already so aroused
we'd become incapable of caution.

Our clothes half opened—we weren't wearing much:
a divine July was ablaze.

Delight of flesh between
those half-opened clothes;
quick baring of flesh—the vision of it
that has crossed twenty-six years
and comes to rest now in this poetry.

OF THE JEWS (A.D. 50)

Painter and poet, runner and discus-thrower,
beautiful as Endymion: Ianthis, son of Antony.
From a family on friendly terms with the Synagogue.

"My most valuable days are those
when I give up the pursuit of sensuous beauty,
when I desert the elegant and severe cult of Hellenism,
with its over-riding devotion
to perfectly shaped, corruptible white limbs,
and become the man I would want to remain forever:
son of the Jews, the holy Jews."

A most fervent declaration on his part: ". . . to remain
    forever
a son of the Jews, the holy Jews."

But he did not remain anything of the kind.
The Hedonism and Art of Alexandria
kept him as their dedicated son.

IMENOS

". . . what should be cherished even more
is the sensual pleasure that is achieved morbidly,
    corruptingly—
it rarely finds the body able to feel what it requires—
that morbidly, corruptingly creates
an erotic intensity that a healthy disposition cannot
    generate. . . ."

Extract from a letter
written by young Imenos (from a patrician family)
notorious in Syracuse for his debauchery
in the debauched times of Michael the Third.

ON BOARD SHIP

It's like him, of course,
this little pencil portrait.

Hurriedly sketched, on the ship's deck,
the afternoon magical,
the Ionian Sea around us.

It's like him. But I remember him as better looking.
He was sensitive almost to the point of illness,
and this highlighted his expression.
He appears to me better looking
now that my soul brings him back, out of Time.

Out of Time. All these things are from very long ago—
the sketch, the ship, the afternoon.

OF DIMITRIOS SOTIR (162-150 B.C.)

Everything he had hoped for turned out wrong!

He had seen himself doing great things,
ending the humiliation that had kept his country down
ever since the battle of Magnesia—
seen himself making Syria a powerful state again,
with her armies, her fleets,
her great fortresses, her wealth.

He had suffered in Rome, become bitter
when he sensed in the talk of friends,
young men of the great families,
that in spite of all their delicacy, their politeness
toward him, the son
of King Selefkos Philopator—
when he sensed that in spite of this there was always
a secret contempt for the Hellenizing dynasties:
their heyday was over, they weren't fit for anything serious,
were completely unable to rule their peoples.
He had cut himself off, had become indignant, and had sworn
it would not be at all the way they thought.
Why, wasn't he himself full of determination?
He would act, he would fight, he would set things right
    again.

If he could only find a way of getting to the East,
only manage to escape from Italy,
then all this strength he feels
inside him, all this energy,
he would pass on to his people.

Only to find himself in Syria!
He was so young when he left his country
he hardly remembered what it looked like.

But in his mind he had always thought of it
as something sacred that you approach reverently,
as a beautiful place unveiled, a vision
of Greek cities and Greek ports.

And now?
               Now despair and sorrow.
They were right, the young men in Rome.
The dynasties born from the Macedonian Conquest
cannot be kept going any longer.

It doesn't matter. He had made the effort,
fought as much as he could.
And in his bleak disillusion
there's one thing only
that still fills him with pride: how even in failure
he shows the world his same indomitable courage.

The rest: they were dreams and wasted energy.
This Syria—it almost seems it isn't his homeland—
this Syria is the country of Valas and Herakleidis.

IF ACTUALLY DEAD

"Where did the Sage withdraw to, where did he disappear?
After his many miracles,
the renown of his teaching
which spread to so many countries,
he suddenly hid himself and nobody knew for certain
what happened to him
(nor did anybody ever see his grave).
Some reported that he died at Ephesus.
But Damis does not record that in his memoir.
Damis says nothing about the death of Apollonios.
Others said that he disappeared at Lindos.
Or maybe the story is true
about his assumption in Crete,
at the ancient sanctuary of Diktynna.
But then again we have that miraculous,
that supernatural apparition of his
before a young student at Tyana.
Maybe the time has not yet come for him to return
and show himself to the world again;
or maybe, transfigured, he moves among us
unrecognized—. But he will come again
as he was, teaching the ways of truth; and then of course
he will bring back the worship of our gods
and our elegant Hellenic rites."

These were the musings of one of the few pagans,
one of the very few still left,
as he sat in his shabby room just after reading
Philostratos' *On Apollonios of Tyana*.
But even he—a trivial and cowardly man—
played the Christian in public and went to church.

It was the time when Justin, known as the elder,
reigned in total piety,
and Alexandria, a godly city,
detested pitiful idolators.

YOUNG MEN OF SIDON (A.D. 400)

The actor they had brought in to entertain them
also recited a few choice epigrams.

The room opened out on the garden,
and a delicate odor of flowers
mingled with the scent
of the five perfumed young Sidonians.

There were readings from Meleager, Krinagoras, Rhianos.
But when the actor recited
"Here lies Aeschylus, the Athenian, son of Euphorion"
(stressing maybe more than he should have
"his renowned valor" and "sacred Marathonian grove"),
a vivacious young man, mad about literature,
suddenly jumped up and said:

"I don't like that quatrain at all.
Sentiments of that kind seem somehow weak.
Give, I say, all your strength to your work,
make it your total concern. And don't forget your work
even in times of trial or when you near your end.
This is what I expect, what I demand of you—
and not that you completely dismiss from your mind
the magnificent art of your tragedies—
your *Agamemnon*, your marvelous *Prometheus*,
your representations of Orestes and Cassandra,
your *Seven Against Thebes*—to set down for your memorial
merely that as an ordinary soldier, one of the herd,
you too fought against Datis and Artaphernis."

TO CALL UP THE SHADES

One candle is enough. Its gentle light
will be more suitable, will be more gracious
when the Shades arrive, the Shades of Love.

One candle is enough. Tonight the room
should not have too much light. In deep reverie,
all receptiveness, and with the gentle light—
in this deep reverie I will form visions
to call up the Shades, the Shades of Love.

DAREIOS

Phernazis the poet is at work
on the crucial part of his epic:
how Dareios, son of Hystaspis,
took over the Persian kingdom.
(It's from him, Dareios, that our glorious king,
Mithridatis, Dionysos and Evpator, descends.)
But this calls for serious thought; Phernazis has to analyze
the feelings Dareios must have had:
arrogance, maybe, and intoxication? No—more likely
a certain insight into the vanities of greatness.
The poet thinks deeply about the question.

But his servant, rushing in, cuts him short
to announce very serious news:
the war with the Romans has begun;
most of our army has crossed the borders.

The poet is dumbfounded. What a disaster!
How can our glorious king,
Mithridatis, Dionysos and Evpator,
bother about Greek poems now?
In the middle of a war—just think, Greek poems!

Phernazis gets all worked up. What bad luck!
Just when he was sure to distinguish himself
with his *Dareios*, sure to silence
his envious critics once and for all.
What a setback, terrible setback to his plans.

And if it's only a setback, that wouldn't be too bad.
But can we really consider ourselves safe in Amisos?

The town isn't very well fortified,
and the Romans are the most awful enemies.

Are we, Cappadocians, really a match for them?
Is it conceivable?
Are we now to pit ourselves against the legions?
Great gods, protectors of Asia, help us.

But through all his distress, all the turmoil,
the poetic idea comes and goes insistently:
arrogance and intoxication—that's the most likely, of course:
arrogance and intoxication are what Dareios must have felt.

ANNA KOMNINA

In the prologue to her *Alexiad*,
Anna Komnina laments her widowhood.

Her soul is all vertigo.
"And I bathe my eyes," she tells us,
"in rivers of tears. . . . Alas for the waves" of her life,
"alas for the revolutions." Sorrow burns her
"to the bones and the marrow and the splitting" of her soul.

But the truth seems to be this power-hungry woman
knew only one sorrow that really mattered;
even if she doesn't admit it, this arrogant Greek woman
had only one consuming pain:
that with all her dexterity,
she never managed to gain the throne,
virtually snatched out of her hands by impudent John.

A BYZANTINE NOBLEMAN IN EXILE
COMPOSING VERSES

The frivolous can call me frivolous.
I've always been most punctilious about
important things. And I insist
that no one knows better than I do
the Holy Fathers, or the Scriptures, or the Canons of the
    Councils.
Whenever he was in doubt,
whenever he had any ecclesiastical problem,
Botaniatis consulted me, me first of all.
But exiled here (may she be cursed, that viper
Irini Doukaina), and incredibly bored,
it is not altogether unfitting to amuse myself
writing six- and eight-line verses,
to amuse myself poeticizing myths
of Hermes and Apollo and Dionysos,
or the heroes of Thessaly and the Peloponnese;
and to compose the most strict iambics,
such as—if you'll allow me to say so—
the intellectuals of Constantinople don't know how to
    compose.
It may be just this strictness that provokes their
    disapproval.

THEIR BEGINNING

Their illicit pleasure has been fulfilled.
They get up and dress quickly, without a word.
They come out of the house separately, furtively;
and as they move along the street a bit unsettled,
it seems they sense that something about them betrays
what kind of bed they've just been lying on.

But what profit for the life of the artist:
tomorrow, the day after, or years later, he'll give voice
to the strong lines that had their beginning here.

THE FAVOR OF ALEXANDER VALAS

I'm not in the least put out that my chariot wheel broke
and I lost that silly race.
I'll drink great wines the whole night long,
lying among lovely roses. Antioch is all mine.
I'm the most celebrated young man in town—
Valas' weakness, he simply adores me.
You'll see, tomorrow they'll say the race wasn't fair
(though if I'd been crude enough to insist on it secretly,
the flatterers would have given first place even to my limping
     chariot).

MELANCHOLY OF JASON KLEANDER, POET IN KOMMAGINI, A.D. 595

The aging of my body and my beauty
is a wound from a merciless knife.
I'm not resigned to it at all.
I turn to you, Art of Poetry,
because you have a kind of knowledge about drugs:
attempts to numb the pain, in Imagination and Language.

It is a wound from a merciless knife.
Bring your drugs, Art of Poetry—
they numb the wound at least for a little while.

DIMARATOS

His subject, "The character of Dimaratos,"
which Porphyry proposed to him in conversation
was outlined by the young sophist as follows
(he planned to develop it rhetorically later):

"First a courtier of King Dareios,
and after that of King Xerxes,
now with Xerxes and his army,
at last Dimaratos will be vindicated.

He'd been treated very unjustly.
He *was* Ariston's son, but his enemies
bribed the oracle brazenly.
And it wasn't enough that they deprived him of his kingship,
but when he finally gave in and decided
to live quietly as a private citizen,
they had to insult him even in front of the people,
they had to humiliate him publicly at the festival.

As a consequence, he serves Xerxes assiduously.
Along with the great Persian army,
he will make it back to Sparta too;
and king once again, how quickly
he will throw him out, how thoroughly
he will shame that schemer Leotychidis.

So now he spends his days full of anxiety,
advising the Persians, explaining
what they should do to conquer Greece.

Much worrying, much thinking, and for this reason
Dimaratos finds his days so burdensome;

much worrying, much thinking, and for this reason
Dimaratos cannot find a moment's joy—
because what he's feeling can't be called joy
(it is not; he will not admit it;
how can he call it joy? His distress could not be greater)
now things make it quite clear to him
that it is the Greeks who are going to win.''

I'VE BROUGHT TO ART

I sit in a mood of reverie.
I brought to Art desires and sensations:
things half-glimpsed,
faces or lines, certain indistinct memories
of unfulfilled love affairs. Let me submit to Art:
Art knows how to shape forms of Beauty,
almost imperceptibly completing life,
blending impressions, blending day with day.

FROM THE SCHOOL OF
THE RENOWNED PHILOSOPHER

For two years he studied with Ammonios Sakkas,
but he was bored by both philosophy and Sakkas.

Then he went into politics.
But he gave that up. That Prefect was an idiot,
and those around him, somber-faced officious nitwits:
their Greek—poor fools—absolutely barbaric.

After that he became
vaguely curious about the Church: to be baptized
and pass as a Christian. But he soon
changed his mind: it would certainly have caused a row
with his parents, ostentatious pagans,
and—horrible thought—
they would have cut off at once
their extremely generous allowance.

But he had to do something. He began to haunt
the corrupt houses of Alexandria,
every secret den of debauchery.

In this fortune favored him:
he'd been given an extremely handsome figure.
And he enjoyed the divine gift.

His looks would last
at least another ten years. And after that?
Maybe he'll go back to Sakkas.
Or if the old man has died meanwhile,
he'll go to another philosopher or sophist:
there's always someone suitable around.

Or in the end he might possibly return
even to politics—commendably remembering
the traditions of his family,
duty toward the country,
and other resonant banalities of that kind.

CRAFTSMAN OF WINE BOWLS

On this wine bowl—pure silver,
made for the house of Herakleidis,
where good taste is the rule—
notice these graceful flowers, the streams, the thyme.
In the center I put this beautiful young man,
naked, erotic, one leg still dangling
in the water. O memory, I begged
for you to help me most in making
the young face I loved appear the way it was.
This proved very difficult because
some fifteen years have gone by since the day
he died as a soldier in the defeat at Magnesia.

THOSE WHO FOUGHT FOR
THE ACHAIAN LEAGUE

Brave men were you who fought and died so nobly,
never afraid of those who were winning every battle.
You were not to blame if Diaios and Kritolaos were at fault.
When Greeks are in a mood to boast, they'll say
"It is men like those our nation breeds."
That's how great their praise will be.

Written by an Achaian in Alexandria
during the seventh year of Ptolemy Lathyros' reign.

TO ANTIOCHOS EPIPHANIS

The young Antiochian said to the king:
"My heart pulses with a precious hope.
The Macedonians, Antiochos Epiphanis,
the Macedonians are back in the great fight.
Let them only win, and I will give anyone who wants them
the lion and the horses, the coral Pan,
the elegant palace, the gardens of Tyre,
and everything else you've given me, Antiochos Epiphanis."

The king may have been moved a little,
but then he remembered his father, his brother,
and said nothing: an eavesdropper
might repeat something they had said. In any case, as
    expected,
the terrible catastrophe came swiftly, at Pydna.

IN AN OLD BOOK

Forgotten between the leaves of an old book—
almost a hundred years old—
I found an unsigned watercolor.
It must have been the work of a powerful artist.
Its title: "Representation of Love."

" . . . love of extreme sensualists" would have been more to
the point.

Because it became clear as you looked at the work
(it was easy to see what the artist had in mind)
that the young man in the painting
was not designated for those
who love in ways that are more or less healthy,
inside the bounds of what is clearly permissible—
with his deep chestnut eyes,
the rare beauty of his face,
the beauty of anomalous charm,
with those ideal lips that bring
sensual delight to the body loved,
those ideal limbs shaped for beds
that common morality calls shameless.

IN DESPAIR

He lost him completely. And he now tries to find
his lips in the lips of each new lover,
he tries in the union with each new lover
to convince himself that it's the same young man,
that it's to him he gives himself.

He lost him completely, as though he never existed.
He wanted, his lover said, to save himself
from the tainted, unhealthy form of sexual pleasure,
the tainted, shameful form of sexual pleasure.
There was still time, he said, to save himself.

He lost him completely, as though he never existed.
Through fantasy, through hallucination,
he tries to find his lips in the lips of other young men,
he longs to feel his kind of love once more.

JULIAN SEEING CONTEMPT

"Observing, then, that there is great contempt for the gods
among us"—he says in his solemn way.
Contempt. But what did he expect?
Let him organize religion as much as he liked,
write to the High Priest of Galatia as much as he liked,
or to others of his kind, inciting them, giving instructions.
His friends weren't Christians; that much was certain.
But even so they couldn't play
as he could (brought up a Christian)
with a new religious system,
ludicrous in both theory and application.
They were, after all, Greeks. Nothing in excess, Augustus.

EPITAPH OF ANTIOCHOS,
KING OF KOMMAGINI

After the funeral of the learned Antiochos, King of
    Kommagini,
whose life had been restrained and gentle,
his sister, deeply afflicted,
wanted an epitaph for him.
So, on the advice of Syrian courtiers,
the Ephesian sophist Kallistratos (who often resided
in the small state of Kommagini
and was a welcome and frequent guest
at the royal house)
wrote an epitaph and sent it to the old lady.

"People of Kommagini, let the glory of Antiochos,
the beneficent king, be celebrated as it deserves.
He was a provident ruler of the country.
He was just, wise, courageous.
In addition he was that best of things, Hellenic—
mankind has no quality more precious:
everything beyond that belongs to the gods."

THEATRE OF SIDON (A.D. 400)

Son of an honorable citizen—most important of all, a
    good-looking
young man of the theatre, amiable in many ways.
I sometimes write highly audacious verses in Greek
and these I circulate—surreptitiously, of course.
O gods, may those puritans who prattle about morals
never see those verses about an exceptional kind of sexual
    pleasure,
the kind that leads toward a condemned, a barren love.

JULIAN IN NICOMEDIA

Things impolitic and dangerous:
praise for Greek ideals,
supernatural magic, visits to pagan temples.
Enthusiasm for the ancient gods.
Frequent talks with Chrysanthios.
Speculation with Maximus, the astute philosopher.
And look what's happened. Gallos is extremely worried.
Konstantios has become suspicious.
Julian's advisors weren't at all prudent.
The matter, says Mardonios, has gone too far,
the talk it has aroused must be stopped at all cost.—
So Julian goes to the church at Nicomedia,
a lector again, and there
with deep reverence he reads out loud
passages from the Holy Scriptures,
and everyone marvels at his Christian piety.

BEFORE TIME ALTERED THEM

They were full of sadness at their parting.
That wasn't what they themselves wanted: it was
    circumstances.
The need to earn a living forced one of them
to go far away—New York or Canada.
The love they felt wasn't, of course, what it once had been;
the attraction between them had gradually diminished,
the attraction had diminished a great deal.
But to be separated, that wasn't what they themselves
    wanted.
It was circumstances. Or maybe Fate
appeared as an artist and parted them now,
before their feeling died out completely, before Time altered
    them:
the one seeming to remain for the other always what he
    was,
the exquisite young man of twenty-four.

HE HAD COME THERE TO READ

He had come there to read. Two or three books lie open,
books by historians, by poets.
But he read for barely ten minutes,
then gave it up, falling half asleep on the sofa.
He's completely devoted to books—
but he's twenty-three, and very good-looking;
and this afternoon Eros entered
his ideal flesh, his lips.
An erotic warmth entered
his completely lovely flesh—
with no ridiculous shame about the form the pleasure
    took. . . .

IN ALEXANDRIA, 31 B.C.

From his village near the outskirts of town,
still dust-covered from the journey in,
the peddler arrives. And ''Incense!'' ''Gum!''
''The best olive oil!'' ''Perfume for your hair!''
he hawks through the streets. But with all the hubbub,
the music, the parades, who can hear him?
The crowd shoves him, drags him along, knocks him around.
And when he asks, now totally confused, ''What's going on
    here?''
someone tosses him too the huge palace lie:
that Antony is winning in Greece.

JOHN KANTAKUZINOS TRIUMPHS

He sees the fields that still belong to him:
the wheat, the animals, the trees laden with fruit;
and beyond them his ancestral home
full of clothes, costly furniture, silverware.

They'll take it all away from him—O God—they'll take it all
    away from him now.

Would Kantakuzinos show pity for him
if he went and fell at his feet? They say he's merciful,
very merciful. But those around him? And the army?—
Or should he fall down and plead before Lady Irini?

Fool that he was to get mixed up in Anna's party!
If only Lord Andronikos had never married her!
Has she ever done anything good, shown any humanity?
Even the Franks don't respect her any longer.
Her plans were ridiculous, all her plotting farcical.
While they were threatening everyone from Constantinople,
Kantakuzinos demolished them, Lord John demolished them.

And to think he'd planned to join Lord John's party!
And he would have done it, and would have been happy now,
a great nobleman still, his position secure,
if the bishop hadn't dissuaded him at the last moment
with his imposing hieratic presence,
his information bogus from beginning to end,
his promises, and all his drivel.

TEMETHOS, ANTIOCHIAN, A.D. 400

Lines written by young Temethos, madly in love.
The title: "Emonidis"—the favorite
of Antiochos Epiphanis; a very handsome young man
from Samosata. But if the lines come out
ardent, full of feeling, it is because Emonidis
(belonging to that other, much older time:
the 137th year of the Greek kingdom,
maybe a bit earlier) is in the poem
merely as a name—a suitable one nevertheless.
The poem gives voice to the love Temethos feels,
a beautiful kind of love, worthy of him. We the initiated—
his intimate friends—we the initiated
know about whom those lines were written.
The unsuspecting Antiochians read simply "Emonidis."

OF COLORED GLASS

I am very moved by one detail
in the coronation at Vlachernai of John Kantakuzinos
and Irini, daughter of Andronikos Asan.
Because they had only a few precious stones
(our afflicted empire was extremely poor)
they wore artificial ones: numerous pieces of glass,
red, green, or blue. I find
nothing humiliating or undignified
in those little pieces of colored glass.
On the contrary, they seem
a sad protest against
the unjust misfortune of the couple being crowned,
symbols of what they deserved to have,
of what surely it was right that they should have
at their coronation—a Lord John Kantakuzinos,
a Lady Irini, daughter of Andronikos Asan.

THE TWENTY-FIFTH YEAR OF HIS LIFE

He goes regularly to the taverna
where they had first met the previous month.
He made inquiries, but they weren't able to tell him anything.
From what they said, he gathered that the person he'd met
    there
was someone completely unknown,
one of the many unknown and shady young types
who dropped in there.
But he still goes to the taverna regularly, at night,
and sits there gazing toward the doorway,
gazing toward the doorway until he's worn out.
Maybe he'll walk in. Tonight maybe he'll turn up.

He does this for nearly three weeks.
His mind is sick with longing.
The kisses are there on his mouth.
His flesh, all of it, suffers unremittingly from desire,
the feel of that other body is on his,
he wants to be joined with it again.

Of course he tries not to give himself away.
But sometimes he almost doesn't care.
Besides, he knows what he's exposing himself to,
he's come to accept it. Quite possibly this life of his
will land him in a devastating scandal.

ON AN ITALIAN SHORE

Kimos, son of Menedoros, a young Greek-Italian,
devotes his life to amusing himself,
like most young men in Greater Greece
brought up in the lap of luxury.

But today, in spite of his nature,
he is preoccupied, dejected. Near the shore
he watches, deeply distressed, as they unload
ships with booty taken from the Peloponnese.

Greek loot: booty from Corinth.

Today certainly it is not right,
it is not possible for the young Greek-Italian
to want to amuse himself in any way.

IN THE BORING VILLAGE

In the boring village where he works—
clerk in a textile shop, very young—
and where he's waiting out the two or three months ahead,
another two or three months until business falls off
so he can leave for the city and plunge headlong
into its action, its entertainment;
in the boring village where he's waiting out the time—
he goes to bed tonight full of sexual longing,
all his youth on fire with the body's passion,
his lovely youth given over to a fine intensity.
And in his sleep pleasure comes to him;
in his sleep he sees and has the figure, the flesh he longed
    for . . .

APOLLONIOS OF TYANA IN RHODES

Apollonios was speaking about
proper education and upbringing
with a young man building a luxury house in Rhodes.
"When I enter a temple,"
said the Tyanian in conclusion, "even if it is a small one,
I would much rather see
a gold and ivory statue there
than find in a large temple a statue of common clay."

"Of common clay": how disgusting—
yet some (who haven't been adequately trained)
are taken in by what's bogus. Those of common clay.

KLEITOS' ILLNESS

Kleitos, a likeable young man,
about twenty-three years old—
with an excellent upbringing, a rare knowledge of Greek—
is seriously ill. He caught the fever
that reaped a harvest this year in Alexandria.

The fever found him already worn out morally
by the pain of knowing that his friend, a young actor,
had stopped loving and wanting him.

He's seriously ill, and his parents are terribly worried.

An old servant who brought him up
is also full of fear for Kleitos' life;
and in her terrible anxiety
she remembers an idol she used to worship
when she was young, before she came there as a maid,
to the house of distinguished Christians, and turned Christian
    herself.
She secretly brings some votive cake, some wine and honey,
and places them before the idol. She chants whatever phrases
she remembers from old prayers: odds and ends. The ninny
doesn't realize that the black demon couldn't care less
whether a Christian gets well or not.

IN A TOWNSHIP OF ASIA MINOR

The news about the outcome of the sea-battle at Actium
was of course unexpected.
But there's no need for us to draft a new proclamation.
The name's the only thing that has to be changed.
There, in the concluding lines, instead of: "Having freed the
    Romans
from Octavius, that disaster,
that parody of a Caesar,"
we'll substitute: "Having freed the Romans
from Antony, that disaster, . . . "
The whole text fits very nicely.

"To the most glorious victor,
matchless in his military ventures,
prodigious in his political operations,
on whose behalf the township ardently wished
for Antony's triumph, . . . "
here, as we said, the substitution: "for Octavius Caesar's
    triumph,
regarding it as Zeus' finest gift—
to this mighty protector of the Greeks,
who graciously honors Greek customs,
who is beloved in every Greek domain,
who clearly deserves exalted praise,
and whose exploits should be recorded at length
in the Greek language, in both verse and prose,
in the *Greek language*, the vehicle of fame,"
et cetera, et cetera. It all fits brilliantly.

PRIEST AT THE SERAPEION

My kind old father
whose love for me has always stayed the same—
I mourn my kind old father
who died two days ago, just before dawn.

Christ Jesus, I try each day
in my every thought, word, and deed
to keep the commandments
of your most holy Church; and I abhor
all who deny you. But now I mourn:
I grieve, O Christ, for my father
even though he was—terrible as it is to say it—
priest at that cursed Serapeion.

IN THE TAVERNAS

I wallow in the tavernas and brothels of Beirut.
I didn't want to stay
in Alexandria. Tamides left me;
he went off with the Prefect's son to earn himself
a villa on the Nile, a mansion in the city.
It wouldn't have been right for me to stay in Alexandria.
I wallow in the tavernas and brothels of Beirut.
I live a vile life, devoted to cheap debauchery.
The one thing that saves me,
like durable beauty, like perfume
that goes on clinging to my flesh, is this: Tamides,
most exquisite of young men, was mine for two years,
and mine not for a house or a villa on the Nile.

A GREAT PROCESSION OF PRIESTS
AND LAYMEN

A procession of priests and laymen—
each walk of life represented—
moves through streets, squares, and gates
of the famous city, Antioch.
At the head of this imposing procession
a handsome white-clad boy
carries the Cross, his arms raised—
our strength and hope, the holy Cross.
The pagans, lately so full of arrogance,
now reticent and cowardly,
quickly slink away from the procession.
Let them keep their distance, always keep their distance from
    us
(as long as they do not renounce their errors).
The holy Cross goes forward; it brings joy and consolation
to every quarter where Christians live;
and these God-fearing people, elated,
stand in their doorways and greet it reverently,
the strength, the salvation of the universe, the Cross.

This is an annual Christian festival.
But today, you see, it is more conspicuous.
The empire is delivered at last.
The vile, the appalling Julian
reigns no longer.

For most pious Jovian let us give our prayers.

SOPHIST LEAVING SYRIA

Eminent sophist, now that you are leaving Syria
with plans to write a book about Antioch,
it's worth your mentioning Mevis in your work—
the famous Mevis, unquestionably
the best looking, the most adored young man
in all Antioch. No one of the others
living his kind of life, no one of them gets paid
what he gets paid. To have Mevis
just for two or three days, they often give
as much as a hundred staters. I said in Antioch;
but in Alexandria as well, in fact in Rome even,
you can't find a young man as attractive as Mevis.

JULIAN AND THE ANTIOCHIANS

*Neither the letter C, they say, nor the
letter K had ever harmed the city. . . . We,
finding interpreters . . . learned that these
are the initial letters of names, the first
of Christ and the second of Konstantios.*

Julian, *Misopogon* (The Beard-Hater)

Was it conceivable that they would ever give up
their beautiful way of life, the range
of their daily pleasures, their brilliant theatre
which consummated a union between Art
and the erotic proclivities of the flesh?

Immoral to a degree—and probably more than a degree—
they certainly were. But they had the satisfaction that their
     life
was the *notorious* life of Antioch,
delectably sensual, in absolute good taste.

To give up all this, indeed, for what?

His hot air about the false gods,
his boring self-advertisement,
his childish fear of the theatre,
his graceless prudery, his ridiculous beard.

O certainly they preferred C,
certainly they preferred K—a hundred times over.

ANNA DALASSINI

In the royal decree that Alexios Komninos
put out especially to honor his mother—
the very intelligent Lady Anna Dalassini,
noteworthy in both her works and her manners—
much is said in praise of her.
Here let me offer one phrase only,
a phrase that is beautiful, sublime:
"She never uttered those cold words 'mine' or 'yours.' "

DAYS OF 1896

He became completely degraded. His erotic tendency,
condemned and strictly forbidden
(but innate for all that), was the cause of it:
society was totally prudish.
He gradually lost what little money he had,
then his social standing, then his reputation.
Nearly thirty, he had never worked a full year—
at least not at a legitimate job.
Sometimes he earned enough to get by
acting the go-between in deals considered shameful.
He ended up the type likely to compromise you thoroughly
if you were seen around with him often.

But this isn't the whole story—that would not be fair.
The memory of his beauty deserves better.
There is another angle; seen from that
he appears attractive, appears
a simple, genuine child of love,
without hesitation putting,
above his honor and reputation,
the pure sensuality of his pure flesh.

Above his reputation? But society,
prudish and stupid, had it wrong.

TWO YOUNG MEN, 23 TO 24 YEARS OLD

He'd been sitting in the café since ten-thirty
expecting him to turn up any minute.
Midnight went by, and he was still waiting for him.
It was now after one-thirty, and the café was almost
    deserted.
He'd grown tired of reading newspapers
mechanically. Of his three lonely shillings
only one was left: waiting that long,
he'd spent the others on coffees and brandy.
He'd smoked all his cigarettes.
So much waiting had worn him out. Because
alone like that for so many hours,
he'd also begun to have disturbing thoughts
about the immoral life he was living.

But when he saw his friend come in—
weariness, boredom, thoughts vanished at once.

His friend brought unexpected news.
He'd won sixty pounds playing cards.

Their good looks, their exquisite youthfulness,
the sensitive love they shared
were refreshed, livened, invigorated
by the sixty pounds from the card table.

Now all joy and vitality, feeling and charm,
they went—not to the homes of their respectable families
(where they were no longer wanted anyway)—
they went to a familiar and very special

house of debauchery, and they asked for a bedroom
and expensive drinks, and they drank again.

And when the expensive drinks were finished
and it was close to four in the morning,
happy, they gave themselves to love.

GREEK FROM ANCIENT TIMES

Antioch is proud of its splendid buildings,
its beautiful streets, the lovely countryside around it,
its teeming population;
proud too of its glorious kings, its artists
and sages, its very rich
yet prudent merchants. But far more
than all this, Antioch is proud to be a city
Greek from ancient times, related to Argos
through Ione, founded by Argive colonists
in honor of Inachos' daughter.

DAYS OF 1901

The exceptional thing about him was
that in spite of all his loose living,
his vast sexual experience,
and the fact that usually
his attitude matched his age,
in spite of this there were moments—
extremely rare, of course—when he gave the impression
that his flesh was almost virginal.

His twenty-nine-year-old beauty,
so tested by sensual pleasure,
would sometimes strangely remind one
of a boy who, somewhat awkwardly, gives
his pure body to love for the first time.

YOU DIDN'T UNDERSTAND

Vacuous Julian had the following to say
about our religious beliefs: "I read, I understood
I condemned." He thought we'd be annihilated
by that "condemned," the silly ass.

Witticisms like that don't cut any ice with us Christians.
Our quick reply: "You read but didn't understand;
had you understood, you wouldn't have condemned."

A YOUNG POET IN HIS
TWENTY-FOURTH YEAR

Brain, work now as well as you can.
A one-sided passion is destroying him.
He's in a maddening situation.
Every day he kisses the face he worships,
his hands are on those exquisite limbs.
He's never loved before with this degree of passion.
But the beautiful fulfillment of love
is lacking, that fulfillment is lacking
which both of them must want with the same intensity.

(They aren't equally given to the abnormal form of sensual
    pleasure;
only he is completely possessed by it.)

And so he's wearing himself out, all on edge.
Then—to make things worse—he's out of work.
He manages somehow to borrow
a little here and there (sometimes
almost begging for it) and he just gets by.
He kisses those adored lips, excites himself
on that exquisite body—though he now feels
it only acquiesces. And then
he drinks and smokes, drinks and smokes;
and he drags himself to the cafés all day long,
drags the weariness consuming his beauty.
Brain, work now as well as you can.

IN SPARTA

He didn't know, King Kleomenis, he didn't dare—
he just did not know how to tell his mother
a thing like this: that Ptolemy demanded,
to guarantee their treaty, that she too go to Egypt
and be held there as a hostage—
a very humiliating, indecorous thing.
And he would be about to speak yet always hesitate,
would start to tell her yet always stop.

But the magnificent woman understood him
(she had already heard some rumors about it)
and she encouraged him to come out with it clearly.
And she laughed, saying of course she would go,
indeed was happy that in her old age
she could be useful to Sparta still.

As for the humiliation—that didn't touch her at all.
Of course an upstart like the Lagid
couldn't possibly comprehend the Spartan spirit;
so his demand could not in fact humiliate
a Royal Lady like herself:
mother of a Spartan king.

PICTURE OF A 23-YEAR-OLD PAINTED BY HIS FRIEND OF THE SAME AGE, AN AMATEUR

He finished the picture yesterday noon.
Now he looks at it detail by detail. He's painted him
wearing an unbuttoned gray jacket,
no vest, tieless, with a rose-colored
shirt, open, allowing a glimpse
of his beautiful chest and neck.
The right side of his forehead is almost covered
by his hair, his lovely hair
(done in the style he's recently adopted).
He's managed to capture perfectly the sensual note
he wanted when he did the eyes,
when he did the lips . . .
That mouth of his, those lips
so ready to satisfy a special kind of erotic pleasure.

A PRINCE FROM WESTERN LIBYA

Aristomenis, son of Menelaos,
the Prince from Western Libya,
was generally liked in Alexandria
during the ten days he spent there.
As his name, his dress, modest, was also Greek.
He received honors gladly,
but he did not solicit them; he was unassuming.
He bought Greek books,
especially history and philosophy.
Above all he was a man of few words.
It got around that he must be a profound thinker,
and men like that naturally don't speak very much.

He was neither a profound thinker nor anything else—
just a piddling, laughable man.
He assumed a Greek name, dressed like the Greeks,
learned to behave more or less like a Greek;
and all the time he was terrified he would spoil
his reasonably good image
by coming out with barbaric howlers in Greek
and the Alexandrians, in their usual way,
would make fun of him, vile people that they are.

This was why he limited himself to a few words,
terribly careful of his syntax and pronunciation;
and he was driven almost out of his mind, having
so much talk bottled up inside him.

KIMON, SON OF LEARCHOS, 22,
STUDENT OF GREEK LITERATURE
(IN KYRINI)

"My end came while I was happy.
Ermotelis had me for his inseparable friend.
During my last days, though he tried to make me believe
that he wasn't worried, I often noticed his eyes
red from crying. And when he'd think
I'd fallen asleep, he'd collapse at the edge of my bed
as though out of his mind. But we were both young men
of the same age, twenty-three years old.
Fate is a traitor. Maybe some other passion
would have taken Ermotelis from me.
I died well: in love that was undivided."

This epitaph for Marylos, son of Aristodimos,
who died in Alexandria a month ago,
was sent to me, his cousin Kimon, in my mourning.
It was sent by the author, a poet friend of mine,
sent because he knew I was related to Marylos—that's all he
  knew.
My heart is full of sorrow over Marylos.
We grew up together, like brothers.
I'm deeply saddened. His premature death
completely wiped out any grudge . . .
any grudge I may have had against Marylos, even if
he did steal Ermotelis' love away from me—
so that if Ermotelis should want me again now,
it won't be at all the same as it was. I know
this susceptible nature of mine. The image of Marylos

will come between us, and I will imagine it
saying to me: ''See, you're satisfied now.
You've taken him back again as you longed to, Kimon;
see, you no longer have an excuse for maligning me now.''

ON THE MARCH TO SINOPI

Mithridatis, glorious and powerful,
ruler of great cities,
master of strong armies and fleets,
on the march to Sinopi took a route
through a remote part of the country
where a soothsayer lived.

Mithridatis sent one of his officers
to ask the soothsayer how much more wealth,
how much more power, he'd accumulate in the future.

He dispatched one of his officers,
then continued his march to Sinopi.

The soothsayer withdrew into a secret room.
About a half an hour later he came out
troubled, and said to the officer:
"I wasn't able to clarify things very well.
Today is not a propitious day—
there were some murky shadows, I didn't understand them
    fully—.
But, I think, the king should be content with what he has.
Anything more will prove dangerous for him.
Remember, officer, to tell him that:
for God's sake to be satisfied with what he has.
Fortune changes suddenly.
Tell King Mithridatis this:
it's extremely rare to come across anyone like his ancestor's
    companion,
that noble companion who wrote in the earth with his lance
those timely words that saved him: 'Escape, Mithridatis.' "

DAYS OF 1909, '10, AND '11

He was the son of a harassed, poverty-stricken sailor
(from an island in the Aegean Sea).
He worked for a blacksmith: his clothes shabby,
his workshoes miserably torn,
his hands filthy with rust and oil.

In the evenings, after the shop closed,
if there was something he longed for especially,
a fairly expensive tie,
a tie for Sunday,
or if he saw and coveted
a beautiful blue shirt in some store window,
he'd sell his body for a dollar or two.

I ask myself if the glorious Alexandria
of ancient times could boast of a boy
more exquisite, more perfect—lost though he was:
that is, we don't have a statue or painting of him;
thrust into that awful blacksmith's shop,
overworked, tormented, given to cheap debauchery,
he was soon used up.

MYRIS: ALEXANDRIA, A.D. 340

When I heard the terrible news, that Myris was dead,
I went to his house, although I avoid
going to the houses of Christians,
especially during times of mourning or festivity.

I stood in the corridor. I didn't want
to go further inside because I noticed
that the relatives of the deceased looked at me
with obvious surprise and displeasure.

They had him in a large room,
and from the corner where I stood
I could catch a glimpse of it: all precious carpets,
and vessels in silver and gold.

I stood and wept in a corner of the corridor.
And I thought how our parties and excursions
would no longer be worthwhile without Myris;
and I thought how I'd no longer see him
at our wonderfully indecent night-long sessions
enjoying himself, laughing, and reciting verses
with his perfect feel for Greek rhythm;
and I thought how I'd lost forever
his beauty, lost forever
the young man I'd worshipped so passionately.

Some old women close to me were talking with lowered
    voices
about the last day he lived:
the name of Christ constantly on his lips,
his hand holding a cross.

Then four Christian priests
came into the room, and said prayers
fervently, and orisons to Jesus,
or to Mary (I'm not very familiar with their religion).

We'd known, of course, that Myris was a Christian,
known it from the very start,
when he first joined our group the year before last.
But he lived exactly as we did.
More devoted to pleasure than all of us,
he scattered his money lavishly on amusements.
Not caring what anyone thought of him,
he threw himself eagerly into night-time scuffles
when our group happened to clash
with some rival group in the street.
He never spoke about his religion.
And once we even told him
that we'd take him with us to the Serapeion.
But—I remember now—
he didn't seem to like this joke of ours.
And yes, now I recall two other incidents.
When we made libations to Poseidon,
he drew himself back from our circle and looked elsewhere.
And when one of us in his fervor said:
"May all of us be favored and protected
by the great, the sublime Apollo"—
Myris, unheard by the others, whispered: "not counting
    me."

The Christian priests were praying loudly
for the young man's soul.

I noticed with how much diligence,
how much intense concern
for the forms of their religion, they were preparing
everything for the Christian funeral.
And suddenly an odd sensation
took hold of me. Indefinably I felt
as if Myris were going from me;
I felt that he, a Christian, was united
with his own people and that I was becoming
a stranger, a total stranger. I even felt
a doubt come over me: that I'd also been deceived by my
    passion
and had always been a stranger to him.
I rushed out of their horrible house,
rushed away before my memory of Myris
could be captured, could be perverted by their Christianity.

ALEXANDER JANNAIOS AND
ALEXANDRA

Full of their success, thoroughly satisfied,
King Alexander Jannaios
and his wife Queen Alexandra
move through the streets of Jerusalem
with musicians in the lead
and every kind of pomp and circumstance.
The work begun by the great Judas Maccabaios
and his four celebrated brothers
has now been concluded brilliantly,
work relentlessly carried on
among so many obstacles and dangers.
Nothing unseemly remains now.
All subservience to the haughty monarchs
of Antioch is over. Clearly
King Alexander Jannaios
and his wife Queen Alexandra
are equal to the Selefkids in every way.
Good Jews, pure Jews, devoted Jews above all.
But, as circumstances require,
also skilled in speaking Greek,
even on familiar terms with Greeks and Hellenized
     monarchs—
as equals, though, let that be understood.
The work begun by the great Judas Maccabaios
and his four celebrated brothers
has indeed been concluded brilliantly,
concluded in the most striking way.

LOVELY WHITE FLOWERS

He went inside the café where they used to go together.
It was here, three months ago, that his friend had told him:
"We're completely broke—the two of us so poor
that we're down to sitting in the cheapest places.
I have to tell you straight out—
I can't go around with you any more.
I want you to know, somebody else is after me."
The "somebody else" had promised him two suits,
some silk handkerchiefs. To get his friend back,
he himself went through hell rounding up twenty pounds.
His friend came back to him for the twenty pounds—
but along with that, for their old intimacy,
their old love, for the deep feeling between them.
The "somebody else" was a liar, a real bum:
he'd ordered only one suit for his friend,
and that under pressure, after much begging.

But now he doesn't want the suits any longer,
he doesn't want the silk handkerchiefs at all,
or twenty pounds, or twenty piasters even.

Sunday they buried him, at ten in the morning.
Sunday they buried him, almost a week ago.

He laid flowers on his cheap coffin,
lovely white flowers, very much in keeping
with his beauty, his twenty-two years.

When he went to the café that evening—
he happened to have some vital business there—the same café
where they used to go together: it was a knife in his heart,
that dingy café where they used to go together.

COME, O KING OF THE LACEDAIMONIANS

Kratisiklia didn't deign to allow
the people to see her weeping and grieving:
she walked in dignity and in silence.
Her calm face betrayed nothing
of her sorrow and her agony.
But even so, for a moment she couldn't hold back:
before she went aboard the detestable ship for Alexandria
she took her son to Poseidon's temple,
and once they were alone
she embraced him tenderly and kissed him
(he was "in great distress," says Plutarch, "badly shaken").
But her strong character struggled through;
regaining her poise, the magnificent woman
said to Kleomenis: "Come, O King of the Lacedaimonians,
when we go outside
let no one see us weeping
or behaving in any way unworthy of Sparta.
At least this is still in our power;
what lies ahead is in the hands of the gods."

And she boarded the ship, going toward whatever lay "in the
hands of the gods."

IN THE SAME SPACE

The setting of houses, cafés, the neighborhood
that I've seen and walked through years on end:

I created you while I was happy, while I was sad,
with so many incidents, so many details.

And, for me, the whole of you is transformed into feeling.

THE MIRROR IN THE FRONT HALL

The luxurious house had a huge mirror
in the front hall, a very old mirror,
bought at least eighty years ago.

A very handsome boy, a tailor's assistant
(on Sundays an amateur athlete),
stood there with a package. He gave it
to one of the household who took it in
to get the receipt. The tailor's assistant
was left alone, waiting there.
He went up to the mirror, looked at himself,
and adjusted his tie. Five minutes later
they brought him the receipt. He took it and went away.

But the old mirror that had seen so much
during a life of many years—
thousands of objects and faces—
the old mirror was all joy now,
proud to have embraced
total beauty for a few moments.

HE ASKED ABOUT THE QUALITY

He left the office where he'd taken up
a trivial, poorly paid job
(eight pounds a month, including bonuses)—
left at the end of the dreary work
that kept him bent all afternoon,
came out at seven and walked off slowly,
idling his way down the street. Good-looking;
and interesting: showing as he did that he'd reached
his full sensual capacity.
He'd turned twenty-nine the month before.

He idled his way down the main street
and the poor side-streets that led to his home.

Passing in front of a small shop
that sold cheap and flimsy things for workers,
he saw a face inside there, saw a figure
that compelled him to go in, and he pretended
he wanted to look at some colored handkerchiefs.

He asked about the quality of the handkerchiefs
and how much they cost, his voice choking,
almost silenced by desire.
And the answers came back the same way,
distracted, the voice hushed,
offering hidden consent.

They kept on talking about the merchandise—but
the only purpose: that their hands might touch
over the handkerchiefs, that their faces, their lips,

might move close together as though by chance—
a moment's meeting of limb against limb.

Quickly, secretly, so the shopowner sitting at the back
wouldn't realize what was going on.

TO HAVE TAKEN THE TROUBLE

I'm broke and practically homeless.
This fatal city, Antioch,
has devoured all my money:
this fatal city with its extravagant life.

But I'm young and in excellent health.
Prodigious master of things Greek,
I know Aristotle and Plato through and through,
poets, orators, or anyone else you could mention.
I have some idea about military matters
and friends among the senior mercenaries.
I also have a foot in the administrative world;
I spent six months in Alexandria last year:
I know (and this is useful) something about what goes on
    there—
the scheming of Kakergetis, his dirty deals, and the rest of it.

So I consider myself completely qualified
to serve this country,
my beloved fatherland, Syria.

Whatever job they give me,
I'll try to be useful to the country. That's my intention.
But if they frustrate me with their maneuvers—
we know them, those smart operators: no need to say more
    here—
if they frustrate me, it's not my fault.

I'll approach Zabinas first,
and if that idiot doesn't appreciate me,
I'll go to his rival, Grypos.

And if that imbecile doesn't take me on,
I'll go straight to Hyrkanos.

One of the three will want me anyway.

And my conscience is quiet
about my not caring which one I chose:
the three of them are equally bad for Syria.

But, a ruined man, it's not my fault.
I'm only trying, poor devil, to make ends meet.
The almighty gods ought to have taken the trouble
to create a fourth, an honest man.
I would gladly have gone along with him.

FOLLOWING THE RECIPE OF ANCIENT
GRECO-SYRIAN MAGICIANS

Said an aesthete: "What distillation from magic herbs
can I find—what distillation, following the recipe
of ancient Greco-Syrian magicians—
that will bring back to me for one day (if its power
doesn't last longer) or even for a few hours,
my twenty-third year,
bring back to me my friend of twenty-two,
his beauty, his love.

What distillation, following the recipe
of ancient Greco-Syrian magicians, can be found
to bring back also—as part of this return of things past—
even the little room we shared."

IN THE YEAR 200 B.C.

"Alexander, son of Philip, and the Greeks except the
    Lacedaimonians . . . "

We can very well imagine
how completely indifferent the Spartans would have been
to this inscription. "Except the Lacedaimonians"—
naturally. The Spartans
weren't to be led and ordered around
like precious servants. Besides,
a pan-Hellenic expedition without
a Spartan king in command
was not to be taken very seriously.
Of course, then, "except the Lacedaimonians."

That's certainly one point of view. Quite understandable.

So, "except the Lacedaimonians" at Granikos,
then at Issus, then in the decisive battle
where the terrible army
the Persians mustered at Arbela was wiped out:
it set out for victory from Arbela, and was wiped out.

And from this marvelous pan-Hellenic expedition,
triumphant, brilliant in every way,
celebrated on all sides, glorified
as no other has ever been glorified,
incomparable, we emerged:
the great new Hellenic world.

We the Alexandrians, the Antiochians,
the Selefkians, and the countless

other Greeks of Egypt and Syria,
and those in Media, and Persia, and all the rest:
with our far-flung supremacy,
our flexible policy of judicious integration,
and our Common Greek Language
which we carried as far as Bactria, as far as the Indians.

Talk about Lacedaimonians after that!

DAYS OF 1908

He was out of work that year,
so he lived off card games,
backgammon, and borrowed money.

He was offered a job at three pounds a month
in a small stationery store,
but he turned it down without the slightest hesitation.
It wasn't suitable. It wasn't the right pay for him,
a reasonably educated young man, twenty-five years old.

He won two, maybe three dollars a day—sometimes.
How much could he expect to make out of cards and
    backgammon
in the cafés of his social level, working-class places,
however cleverly he played, however stupid the opponents he
    chose?
His borrowing—that was even worse.
He rarely picked up a dollar, usually no more than half that,
and sometimes he had to come down to even less.

For a week or so, sometimes longer,
when he managed to escape those horrible late nights,
he'd cool himself at the baths, and with a morning swim.

His clothes were a terrible mess.
He always wore the same suit,
a very faded cinnamon-brown suit.

O summer days of nineteen hundred and eight,
from your perspective
the cinnamon-brown suit was tastefully excluded.

Your perspective has preserved him
as he was when he took off, threw off,
those unworthy clothes, that mended underwear,
and stood stark naked, impeccably handsome, a miracle—
his hair uncombed, swept back,
his limbs a little tanned
from his morning nakedness at the baths and on the beach.

''UNPUBLISHED POEMS''
1896-1933

JULIAN AT THE MYSTERIES

But when he found himself in darkness,
in the earth's dreadful depths,
accompanied by unholy Greeks,
and bodiless figures appeared before him
with haloes and bright lights,
the young Julian momentarily lost his nerve:
an impulse from his pious years came back
and he crossed himself.
The Figures vanished at once;
the haloes faded away, the lights went out.
The Greeks exchanged glances.
The young man said: "Did you see the miracle?
Dear companions, I'm frightened.
I'm frightened, friends. I want to leave.
Didn't you see how the demons vanished
the second they saw me make
the holy sign of the cross?"
The Greeks chuckled scornfully:
"Shame on you, shame, to talk that way
to us sophists and philosophers!
If you want to say things like that,
say them to the Bishop of Nicomedia
and his priests.
The greatest gods of our glorious Greece
appeared before you.
And if they left, don't think for a minute
that they were frightened by a gesture.
It was just that when they saw you
making that vile, that crude sign,
their noble nature was disgusted
and they left you in contempt."

This is what they said to him,
and the fool recovered from
his holy, blessed fear, convinced
by the unholy words of the Greeks.

KING CLAUDIUS

My mind now moves to distant places.
I'm walking the streets of Elsinore,
through its squares, and I recall
the very sad story
of that unfortunate king
killed by his nephew
because of some fanciful suspicions.

In all the homes of the poor
he was mourned secretly
(they feared Fortinbras).
He was a quiet, gentle man,
a man who loved peace
(his country had suffered much
from the wars of his predecessor),
he behaved graciously toward everyone,
humble and great alike.
Never high-handed, he always sought advice
in the kingdom's affairs
from serious, experienced people.

Just why his nephew killed him
was never precisely explained.
The prince suspected him of murder,
and the basis of his suspicion was this:
walking one night along an ancient battlement
he thought he saw a ghost
and he had a conversation with this ghost;
what he supposedly heard from the ghost
were certain accusations against the king.

It must have been a fit of fancy,
an optical illusion,
(the prince was highly strung in the extreme;
while he was studying at Wittenberg,
many of his fellow students thought him a maniac).

A few days later he went
to his mother's room to discuss
certain family affairs. And suddenly,
while he was talking, he lost his self-control,
started shouting, screaming
that the ghost was there in front of him.
But his mother saw nothing at all.

And that same day, for no apparent reason,
he killed an old gentleman of the court.
Since the prince was due to sail for England
in a day or two,
the king hustled him off posthaste
in order to save him.
But the people were so outraged
by the monstrous murder
that rebels rose up
and tried to storm the palace gates,
led by the dead man's son,
the noble lord Laertes
(a brave young man, also ambitious;
in the confusion, some of his friends called out:
"Long live King Laertes!").

Later, once the kingdom had calmed down
and the king was lying in his grave,

killed by his nephew (the prince,
who never went to England
but escaped from the ship on his way there),
a certain Horatio came forward
and tried to exonerate the prince
by telling some stories of his own.
He said that the voyage to England
had been a secret plot, and orders
had been given to kill the prince there
(but this was never clearly ascertained).
He also spoke of poisoned wine,
wine poisoned by the king.
It's true that Laertes spoke of this too.
But couldn't he have been lying?
Couldn't he have been mistaken?
And when did he say all this?
While dying of his wounds, his mind reeling,
his talk seemingly babble.
As for the poisoned weapons,
it was shown later that the poisoning
hadn't been done by the king at all:
Laertes had done it by himself.
But Horatio, whenever pressed,
would produce even the ghost as a witness:
the ghost said this and that,
the ghost did this and that!

Because of all this, though hearing Horatio out,
most people in all conscience
pitied the good king,
who, with all these ghosts and fairy tales,
was unjustly killed and disposed of.

Yet Fortinbras, who profited from it all
and gained the throne so easily,
gave full attention and great weight
to every word Horatio said.

WHEN THE WATCHMAN SAW THE LIGHT

Winter, summer, the watchman sat there looking out
from the roof of Atreus' palace. Now he has
good news to report. In the distance he saw the fire light up.
And he's happy; besides, the drudgery's over now.
It's hard to sit there night and day
in heat and cold, looking out for a fire to appear
on the peak of Arachnaion. Now the longed-for signal
has appeared. Yet when happiness
comes, it brings less joy
than one expected. But at least
this much has been gained: we've rid ourselves
of hope and expectation. Many things will happen
to the house of Atreus. No need to be wise
to guess this now the watchman
has seen the light. So let's not exaggerate.
The light is good; and those coming are good,
their words and actions also good.
And let's hope all goes well. But
Argos can do without the house
of Atreus. Ancient houses are not eternal.
Of course many people will have much to say.
We should listen. But we won't be deceived
by words such as Indispensable, Unique, and Great.
Someone else indispensable and unique and great
can always be found at a moment's notice.

GROWING IN SPIRIT

He who hopes to grow in spirit
will have to transcend obedience and respect.
He will hold to some laws
but he will mostly violate
both law and custom, and go beyond
the established, inadequate norm.
Sensual pleasures will have much to teach him.
He will not be afraid of the destructive act:
half the house will have to come down.
This way he will grow virtuously into wisdom.

SEPTEMBER, 1903

At least let me now deceive myself with illusions
so as not to feel my empty life.

And yet I came so close so many times.
And yet how paralyzed I was, how cowardly;
why did I keep my lips sealed
while my empty life wept inside me,
my desires wore robes of mourning?

To have been so close so many times
to those sensual eyes, those lips,
to that body I dreamed of, loved.
To have been so close so many times.

DECEMBER, 1903

And if I cannot speak about my love—
if I do not talk about your hair, your lips, your eyes,
still your face that I keep within my heart,
the sound of your voice that I keep within my mind,
the days of September that rise in my dreams,
give shape and color to my words, my sentences,
whateve: theme I touch, whatever thought I utter.

ON THE STAIRS

As I was going down those ill-famed stairs
you were coming in the door, and for a second
I saw your unfamiliar face and you saw mine.
Then I hid so you wouldn't see me again, and you
hurried past me, hiding your face,
and slipped inside the ill-famed house
where you couldn't have found sensual pleasure any more
    than I did.

And yet the love you were looking for, I had to give you;
the love I was looking for—so your tired,
knowing eyes implied—you had to give me.
Our bodies sensed and sought each other;
our blood and skin understood.

But, flustered, we both hid ourselves.

AT THE THEATRE

I got bored looking at the stage
and raised my eyes to the box circle.
In one of the boxes I saw you
with your strange beauty, your dissolute youthfulness.
My thoughts turned back at once
to all they'd told me about you that afternoon;
my mind and body were aroused.
And as I gazed enthralled
at your languid beauty, your languid youthfulness,
your tastefully discriminating dress,
in my imagination I kept picturing you
the way they'd talked about you that afternoon.

POSEIDONIANS

*[We behave like] the Poseidonians in the
Tyrrhenian Gulf, who although of Greek
origin, became barbarized as Tyrrhenians
or Romans and changed their speech and
the customs of their ancestors. But they
observe one Greek festival even to this
day; during this they gather together and
call up from memory their ancient names
and customs, and then, lamenting loudly
to each other and weeping, they go away.*

Athenaios, *Deipnosophistai.* Book 14,
31A (632)

The Poseidonians forgot the Greek language
after so many centuries of mingling
with Tyrrhenians, Latins, and other foreigners.
The only thing surviving from their ancestors
was a Greek festival, with beautiful rites,
with lyres and flutes, contests and wreaths.
And it was their habit toward the festival's end
to tell each other about their ancient customs
and once again to speak Greek names
that only a few of them still recognized.
And so their festival always had a melancholy ending
because they remembered that they too were Greeks,
they too once upon a time were citizens of Magna Graecia;
and how low they'd fallen now, what they'd become,
living and speaking like barbarians,
cut off so disastrously from the Greek way of life.

ANTONY'S ENDING

But when he heard the women weeping,
lamenting his sorry state—
madam with her oriental gestures
and her slaves with their barbarized Greek—
the pride in his soul rose up,
his Italian blood sickened with disgust
and all he had worshipped blindly till then—
his passionate Alexandrian life—
now seemed dull and alien.
And he told them "to stop weeping for him,
that kind of thing was all wrong.
They ought to be singing his praises
for having been a great ruler,
so rich in worldly goods.
And if he'd fallen now, he hadn't fallen humbly,
but as a Roman vanquished by a Roman."

HIDDEN THINGS

From all I did and all I said
let no one try to find out who I was.
An obstacle was there that changed the pattern
of my actions and the manner of my life.
An obstacle was often there
to stop me when I'd begin to speak.
From my most unnoticed actions,
my most veiled writing—
from these alone will I be understood.
But maybe it isn't worth so much concern,
so much effort to discover who I really am.
Later, in a more perfect society,
someone else made just like me
is certain to appear and act freely.

ON HEARING OF LOVE

On hearing about powerful love, respond, be moved
like an aesthete. Only, fortunate as you've been,
remember how much your imagination created for you.
This first, and then the rest—the lesser loves—
that you experienced and enjoyed
in your life: the more real and tangible.
Of loves like these you were not deprived.

"THE REST I WILL TELL TO THOSE
DOWN IN HADES"

"Indeed," said the proconsul, closing the book,
"this line is beautiful and very true.
Sophocles wrote it in a deeply philosophic mood.
How much we'll tell down there, how much,
and how very different we'll appear.
What we protect here like sleepless guards,
wounds and secrets locked inside us,
protect with such great anxiety day after day,
we'll disclose freely and clearly down there."

"You might add," said the sophist, half smiling,
"*if* they talk about things like that down there,
if they bother about them any more."

THE PHOTOGRAPH

In this obscene photograph sold secretly
in the street (so the policeman won't see)
in this lewd photograph,
how could there be such a dream-like face?
How did you get in there?

Who knows what a degrading, vulgar life you lead;
how horrible the surroundings must have been
when you posed to have this picture taken;
what a cheap soul you must have.
But in spite of all this, and even more, you remain for me
the dream-like face, the figure
shaped for and dedicated to the Greek kind of sensual
    pleasure—
that's how you remain for me
and how my poetry speaks about you.

GOING BACK HOME FROM GREECE

Well, we're nearly there, Hermippos.
Day after tomorrow, it seems—that's what the captain said.
At least we're sailing our seas,
the waters of Cyprus, Syria, and Egypt,
the beloved waters of our home countries.
Why so silent? Ask your heart:
didn't you too feel happier
the farther we got from Greece?
What's the point of fooling ourselves?
That would hardly be properly Greek.

It's time we admitted the truth:
we are Greeks also—what else are we?—
but with Asiatic affections and feelings,
affections and feelings
sometimes alien to Hellenism.

It isn't right, Hermippos, for us philosophers
to be like some of our petty kings
(remember how we laughed at them
when they used to come to our lectures?)
who through their showy Hellenified exteriors,
Macedonian exteriors (naturally),
let a bit of Arabia peep out now and then,
a bit of Media they can't keep back.
And to what laughable lengths the fools went
trying to cover it up!

No, that's not at all right for us.
For Greeks like us that kind of pettiness won't do.
We must not be ashamed
of the Syrian and Egyptian blood in our veins;
we should really honor it, take pride in it.

EXILES

It goes on being Alexandria still. Just walk a bit
along the straight road that ends at the Hippodrome
and you'll see palaces and monuments that will amaze you.
Whatever war-damage it has suffered,
however much smaller it has become,
it is still a wonderful city.
And then, what with excursions and books
and various kinds of study, time does go by.
In the evenings we meet on the sea front,
the five of us (all, naturally, under fictitious names)
and some other Greeks of the few still left in the city.
Sometimes we discuss church affairs
(the people here seem to lean toward Rome)
and sometimes literature.
The other day we read some lines by Nonnos:
what imagery, what diction, what rhythm and harmony!
All enthusiasm, how we admired the Panopolitan.
So the days go by, and our stay here
is not unpleasant because, naturally,
it is not going to last forever.
We've had good news: either something
is now afoot in Smyrna, or
in April our friends are sure to move from Epiros.
So one way or another, our plans are definitely working
    out,
and we'll easily overthrow Basil.
And when we do, at last our turn will come.

THEOPHILOS PALAIOLOGOS

This is the last year, this the last
of the Greek emperors. And, alas,
how sadly those around him talk.
Kyr Theophilos Palaiologos
in his grief, in his despair, says:
"I would rather die than live."

Ah, Kyr Theophilos Palaiologos,
how much of the pathos, the yearning of our race,
how much weariness
(such exhaustion from injustice and persecution)
your six tragic words contained.

AND I LOUNGED AND LAY
ON THEIR BEDS

When I went to that house of pleasure
I didn't stay in the front rooms where they celebrate,
with some decorum, the accepted modes of love.

I went into the secret rooms
and lounged and lay on their beds.

I went into the secret rooms
considered shameful even to name.
But not shameful to me—because if they were,
what kind of poet, what kind of artist would I be?
I'd rather be an ascetic. That would be more in keeping,
much more in keeping with my poetry,
than for me to find pleasure in the commonplace rooms.

HALF AN HOUR

I never had you, nor I suppose
will I ever have you. A few words, an approach,
as in the bar the other day—nothing more.
It's sad, I admit. But we who serve Art,
sometimes with the mind's intensity,
can create—but of course only for a short time—
pleasure that seems almost physical.
That's how in the bar the other day—
mercifully helped by alcohol—
I had half an hour that was totally erotic.
And I think you understood this
and stayed slightly longer on purpose.
That was very necessary. Because
with all the imagination, with all the magic alcohol,
I needed to see your lips as well,
needed your body near me.

SIMEON

Yes, I know his new poems;
all Beirut is raving about them.
I'll study them some other day.
I can't today because I'm rather upset.

Certainly he's more learned in Greek than Libanius.
A better poet than Meleager though? I don't think so.

But Mevis, why talk about Libanius and books
and all these trivialities? Mevis, yesterday I found myself
(it happened by chance) under Simeon's pillar.

I slipped in among the Christians
praying and worshipping in silence there,
revering him. Not being a Christian myself
I couldn't share their spiritual peace—
I trembled all over and suffered;
I shuddered, disturbed, terribly moved.

Please don't smile; for thirty-five years—think of it—
winter and summer, night and day, for thirty-five years
he's been living and suffering on top of a pillar.
Before either of us was born (I'm twenty-nine,
you must be younger than I am),
before we were born, just imagine it.
Simeon climbed up his pillar
and has stayed there ever since facing God.

I'm in no mood for work today—
but Mevis, I think it better that you report this:
whatever the other sophists may say,
I at least recognize Lamon
as Syria's leading poet.

THE BANDAGED SHOULDER

He said he'd hurt himself against a wall or had fallen down.
But there was probably some other reason
for the wounded, the bandaged shoulder.

Because of a rather abrupt gesture,
as he reached for a shelf to bring down
some photographs he wanted to look at,
the bandage came undone and a little blood ran.

I did it up again, taking my time
over the binding; he wasn't in pain
and I liked looking at the blood.
It was a thing of my love, that blood.

When he left, I found, in front of his chair,
a bloody rag, part of the dressing,
a rag to be thrown straight into the garbage;
and I put it to my lips
and kept it there a long while—
the blood of love against my lips.

ON THE OUTSKIRTS OF ANTIOCH

We in Antioch were astonished when we heard
what Julian was up to now.

Apollo had made things clear to him at Daphni:
he didn't want to give an oracle (as though we cared!),
he didn't intend to speak prophetically, unless
his temple at Daphni was purified first.
The nearby dead, he declared, got on his nerves.

There are many tombs at Daphni.
One of those buried there
was the triumphant and holy martyr Vavylas,
wonder and glory of our church.

It was him the false god hinted at, him he feared.
As long as he felt him near he didn't dare
pronounce his oracle: not a murmur.
(The false gods are terrified of our martyrs.)

Unholy Julian got worked up,
lost his temper and shouted: ''Raise him, carry him out,
take him away immediately, this Vavylas.
You there, do you hear? He gets on Apollo's nerves.
Grab him, raise him at once,
dig him out, take him away, throw him out,
take him wherever you want. This isn't a joke.
Apollo said the temple has to be purified.''

We took it, the holy relic, and carried it elsewhere.
We took it, we carried it away in love and in honor.

And hasn't the temple done brilliantly since!
In no time at all a colossal fire
broke out, a terrible fire,
and both the temple and Apollo burned to nothing.

Ashes the idol: dirt to be swept away.

Julian exploded, and he spread it around—
what else could he do?—that we, the Christians,
had set the fire. Let him say so.
It hasn't been proved. Let him say so.
The essential thing is—he exploded.

EDITOR'S INTRODUCTION
TO THE NOTES

THE TASK of editing Cavafy's poems in translation is relatively simple. The editor has to make sure that the translators have used a reliable text, that the translations are presented in a correct sequence, and that the Greekless reader is provided with notes containing relevant, essential information.

The text used for the first section of this book is that of my two-volume edition of Cavafy's 154 poems, Ποιήματα (1963). The second section is a selection drawn from my edition of his "unpublished poems," Ανέκδοτα Ποιήματα (1968).[1] Both were published in Athens by the Ikaros Publishing Company.

In each section, the poems are presented in chronological order: the "Published Poems" in order of first publication of the final version,[2] mainly as established by Cavafy himself in the chronological tables he attached to his private editions of these poems; and the "Unpublished Poems" in order of composition, as established mainly by Cavafy's own catalogues of poems written from 1891 to 1925. I hasten to add that any attempt to arrange the "Published Poems" in order of *composition* would be not only problematic but in many cases hopeless, partly because the composition dates of most of the thirty-eight poems printed by Cavafy between 1925 and 1932 are not known.

As regards the order of the "Published Poems," the reader may notice that the sequence within each year of publication,

---

[1] With one exception: "On the Outskirts of Antioch," which is included as an appendix in the second volume of the 1963 edition.

[2] Except for "The Funeral of Sarpedon" (see the note to that poem).

and in the initial part subtitled (by Cavafy) "Before 1911," is not quite the same as that adopted by other translators (e.g., the late John Mavrogordato in 1951 or Miss Rae Dalven in 1961). The reason for this difference is that, until 1963, all Greek and foreign editions of Cavafy's poems followed the somewhat arbitrary chronological sequence of the first posthumous edition (1935), a sequence I believe to have been dictated by the "artistic" layout. That same edition—which was the first to be offered for sale to the general public—included the first publication of Cavafy's last completed poem, "On the Outskirts of Antioch," which has now been placed at the end of our second section, i.e., the one containing poems that Cavafy did not publish during his lifetime.

A more significant difference is that between the chronological order adopted here for the poems published up to the end of 1918 and the thematic sequence followed by the equivalent first volume of my 1963 edition of Cavafy's poems.[3] Without going into elaborate bibliographical detail, let me say simply that by the end of his life, Cavafy (according to a practice he had begun to develop at least as early as 1898) chose to distribute the main *corpus* of his poetry in the form of two booklets entitled *Poems: 1905-1915* and *Poems: 1916-1918*, both arranged thematically, and one folder of printed broadsheets, in chronological order of publication, entitled *Poems: 1919-1932*. Although Cavafy's thematic arrangement of the first eighty-four poems is clearly of prime importance for any critical reading of his poetry—as in the similar cases of Baudelaire's *Les Fleurs du Mal* or Emily Dickinson's fascicles—its preservation in a one-volume edition which pre-

---

[3] I have retained the same sequence in my 1991 two-volume edition.

sented the other seventy poems chronologically was thought
to be confusing.[4] So, for the more demanding reader, I have
provided, in an appendix to this introduction, a list of the con-
tents of the 1905-1915 and 1916-1918 booklets (printed in
1930 and 1929 respectively), showing Cavafy's final, pains-
takingly devised thematic order.

The notes that follow are based on the notes to my 1963
and 1968 editions, as well as those to the 1975 edition of the
present volume, supplemented by the notes to my 1991 Greek
edition of the 154 poems (also published by Ikaros). Those in
the former owe much to the publications of George Brissi-
mitzakis, G. Lechonitis, Timos Malanos, John Mavrogor-
dato, G. Papoutsakis, Filippo Maria Pontani, J. A. Sareyan-
nis, George Seferis, A. Singopoulo, and Marguerite
Yourcenar. I have also made use of the notes to *Passions and
Ancient Days* (1971, translated by Edmund Keeley and my-
self), and those to *Selected Poems* (1972, translated by Ed-
mund Keeley and Philip Sherrard), as well as of some hitherto
unpublished material from the Cavafy Papers.

Each poem has its own separate notes, which include the
following:

A. The dates of composition (when known) and first pub-
lication in Greek. Where I use the word "rewritten," I mean
that the poem was actually recast by Cavafy in terms of both
diction and sometimes metre, and not merely corrected in
places, as was often the case with poems even after the pub-
lication of their "definitive" versions. Also, where I use the
word "printed" instead of "published," I mean that the

---

[4] The same argument prevailed in my one-volume *de luxe* edition of Cavafy's
poems (1966), illustrated by Ghika and published in Athens by Ikaros.

poem was first privately printed by Cavafy, usually in broadsheets, and later published in a periodical or literary annual.

B. Any striking metrical characteristics of the original text (not reproduced by the present translators) departing from Cavafy's norm, which is *vers libéré* consisting of unrhymed iambic lines varying from ten to seventeen syllables. I did not think it appropriate in this context to go into the finer (and still mostly unexplored) details of Cavafy's metrical craftsmanship, e.g., rhythmical repetition, enjambment, assonance, sound texture, or even punctuation.

C. Some supplementary information (especially mythological or historical) which might be necessary to the reader, with helpful cross-references. The cross-references are limited, on the whole, to recurring mythological and historical names.[5] Had they been extended to include other related subjects or themes, the notes would have become both subjective and cumbersome.[6] On the other hand, I have referred sparingly to an early thematic catalogue in which Cavafy listed titles of his poems under headings such as: Prisons, Fleeting Years, Our Art, Ancient Days, Passions, the Beginnings of Christianity, Byzantine Days (in fact, I mention such listings only under the first four headings, which are perhaps less obvious than the rest).

I have not attempted to trace Cavafy's literary and histori-

---

[5] For obvious reasons of consistency, I have adopted the spelling used by the translators.

[6] E.g., a simple poem like "Prayer" could involve reference to at least the following thematic categories, which are all present in various other poems by Cavafy: sea, sailor, death by water, young dead, mother, ignorance of reality, Christian religion, holy effigy, candle, homeward journey, prayer, divine compassion, and human hopes versus godly omniscience.

cal sources, except in the case of unattributed direct quotations. Also, chiefly for reasons of space, I have largely abandoned my original intention of quoting his own comments concerning various of his poems: even if most of these Anglo-Greek comments were not as yet undeciphered and/or untranslated,[7] their inclusion here would have increased beyond all manageable proportions the already considerable bulk of these notes.

G.P.S.

Athens, December 1991

Both this Introduction and the Notes are gratefully dedicated to the memory of Patrick Wilkinson, of King's College, Cambridge, who encouraged me to write my first essay on Cavafy.

[7] Their publication by Dr. Diana Haas was first announced in 1983.

215

APPENDIX

I. Poems 1905-1915

1. The City
2. The Satrapy
3. But the Wise Perceive
   Things About to Happen
4. The Ides of March
5. Things Ended
6. The God Abandons
   Antony
7. Theodotos
8. Monotony
9. Ithaka
10. As Much as You Can
11. Trojans
12. King Dimitrios
13. The Glory of the Ptolemies
14. The Retinue of Dionysos
15. The Battle of Magnesia
16. The Displeasure of
    Selefkidis
17. Orophernis
18. Alexandrian Kings
19. Philhellene

20. The Footsteps
21. Herodis Attikos
22. Sculptor of Tyana
23. Tomb of the Grammarian
    Lysias
24. Tomb of Evrion
25. That's the Man
26. Dangerous Thoughts
27. Manuel Komninos
28. In Church
29. Very Seldom
30. For the Shop
31. Pictured
32. Morning Sea
33. Ionic
34. At the Café Door
35. One Night
36. Come Back
37. Long Ago
38. He Swears
39. I Went
40. Chandelier

II. Poems 1916-1918

1. Since Nine O'Clock
2. Understanding
3. Before the Statue of
   Endymion

4. Envoys from Alexandria
5. Aristovoulos
6. Kaisarion
7. Nero's Deadline

8. In the Harbor-Town
9. One of Their Gods
10. Tomb of Lanis
11. Tomb of Iasis
12. In a Town of Osroini
13. Tomb of Ignatios
14. In the Month of Athyr
15. For Ammonis, Who Died
   at 29, in 610
16. Aimilianos Monai,
   Alexandrian, A.D.
   628-655
17. When They Come Alive

18. To Sensual Pleasure
19. I've Looked So Much . . .
20. In the Street
21. The Window of the
   Tobacco Shop
22. Passing Through
23. In the Evening
24. Gray
25. Outside the House
26. The Next Table
27. Body, Remember . . .
28. Days of 1903

III. The following list gives the titles of those poems published before 1905 and not rejected by Cavafy, in the thematic order devised by the poet for his first privately printed collection of poems (1904):

1. Voices
2. Longings
3. Candles
4. An Old Man
5. Prayer
6. The Souls of Old Men
7. The First Step
8. Interruption
9. Thermopylae

10. "Che Fece . . . II Gran
   Rifiuto"
11. The Windows
12. Walls[1]
13. Waiting for the Barbarians
14. Unfaithfulness
15. The Funeral of Sarpedon
16. The Horses of Achilles

[1] This poem was not included in the 1904 edition nor in its enlarged successor privately printed in 1910; its place in the thematic sequence was determined by Cavafy after 1927 in an autograph copy of the 1910 edition, published in facsimile in 1968.

NOTES TO THE POEMS

WALLS   p. 3

Written September 1, 1896, and listed under the heading "Prisons."

Printed probably January 16, 1897, as a private pamphlet containing the Greek text and its English translation, by the poet's brother John, with an epigraph ("How I do suffer unjust things") from Aeschylus' *Prometheus Bound*, 1093.

Couplets of 14-15, 14-15, 15-15, and 15-15 syllables, homophonously rhymed *ab ab cd cd*.

Though certainly never rejected by Cavafy, as were so many of the early compositions he published between 1886 and 1898, this poem was not included in his privately printed collections of 1904 and 1910.

AN OLD MAN   p. 4

Written October 1894, and listed under the heading "Fleeting Years."

Published December 1897, under the heading "Eheu fugaces" = "Alas, the fleeting [years]" (Horace, *Odes*, II, 14).

The line lengths vary from eleven to fourteen syllables, but the second line of each tercet invariably has thirteen syllables; the rhyme scheme is *aab ccd dde ffe ggh iih*.

THE HORSES OF ACHILLES   p. 5

Written July 1896.

Published December 1897, under the heading "Ancient Days."

Both stanzas follow an almost identical metrical pattern: 11-13-13-13-13-17-13 (or 15)-15-15-10-16 syllables; the rhyme scheme is *abbccddaaee* and *fgghhiiffee*.

Patroklos (see "The Funeral of Sarpedon") was the close friend of Achilles (see "Unfaithfulness" and "Trojans"), the son of Peleus and Thetis (see "Interruption" and "Unfaithfulness"). In 1893 Cavafy wrote another poem inspired by the *Iliad*, "Priam's Nocturnal Ride" (not translated here), which remained unpublished until 1968.

PRAYER   p. 6

Written July 1896.

Printed October 23, 1898, as a private pamphlet.

Couplets of 13-13, 12-14, 12-14, and 13-15 syllables, rhymed homophonously (except for the last) *aa bb cc dd*.

THE FUNERAL OF SARPEDON   p. 7

Probably first written before November 1892.

First published December 1898, under the heading "Ancient Days."

Rewritten in August 1908.

Published in September 1908.

This poem, though never actually rejected by Cavafy (who published a final version of it in 1924), was not included in his mature collections *Poems: 1908-1914* (1920), *Poems: 1907-1915* (1926), and *Poems: 1905-1915* (1930); i.e., unlike "The Footsteps" (first published in 1897, and also rewritten in 1908 and published in 1909), it seems still to have been considered by him as a poem belonging to 1898.

Sarpedon, king of Lycia, was killed by Patroklos (see "The Horses of Achilles"), son of Menoitios. Apollo reappears in "Unfaithfulness" and "On the Outskirts of Antioch," and is mentioned in "A Byzantine Nobleman . . ." and "Myris . . ."

CANDLES p. 9

Written August 1893, and listed under the heading "Fleeting Years."

Published December 1899.

THE FIRST STEP p. 10

Written February 1895, entitled "The Last Step," and listed under the heading "Our Art."

Published December 1899.

In eleven-syllable lines.

The scene and Eumenes are probably invented; Theocritus is the Greek poet (fl. c. 270 B.C.) famed for his "idylls" or mainly pastoral dialogues in verse; born in Sicily, he spent part of his life in Alexandria.

THE SOULS OF OLD MEN p. 11

Written August 1898, and listed under the heading "Prisons."

Published December 1901.

In lines of 13-10-10-15-15-10-12-13 syllables, rhymed *abbccdda*.

CHE FECE . . . IL GRAN RIFIUTO p. 12

Written July 1899.

Published August 31, 1901.

The metrical pattern is 13-10-10-15 and 15-10-10-13 syllables, rhymed *abba* and *cddc*.

The title is taken from Dante's *Inferno*, III, 60, and means "He who made . . . the great refusal." Cavafy deliberately omits the words "per viltà" (= "because of cowardice").

INTERRUPTION   p. 13

Written May 1900.
Published December 1901.
The metrical pattern is 12-12-13-14-14-13-13-13 syllables, rhymed *aabccbdd*.

Achilles and Demophon did not become immortal because Achilles' father, Peleus, king of Phthia, and Demophon's mother, Metaneira, queen of Eleusis, prevented the sea-goddess Thetis (see "Unfaithfulness") and the earth-goddess Demetra respectively from completing the fire ritual that would have rendered the two babies invulnerable.

THE WINDOWS   p. 14

Written August 1897, and listed under the heading "Prisons."
Published November 30, 1903.
The metrical pattern is 12-12-13-13-14-14-13-13 syllables, rhymed *aabcddcb* (the *a* and *d* rhymes are almost identical).

THERMOPYLAE   p. 15

Written January 1901.
Published November 30, 1903.
In eleven-syllable lines.

Ephialtis was the Greek traitor who guided a section of the Medes (i.e., the Persian army) over a mountain path to attack the rear of the Greek forces defending the pass of Thermopylae under the leadership of the Spartan king Leonidas (480 B.C.).

UNFAITHFULNESS   p. 16

Written May 1903.
Published May 31, 1904.

In thirteen-syllable lines.

For the main characters, see "The Horses of Achilles," "The Funeral of Sarpedon," "Interruption," and the notes to these poems.

WAITING FOR THE BARBARIANS   p. 18

Written November 1898.

Printed December (?) 1904, as a private pamphlet.

The questions are all in fifteen-syllable lines, the answers mostly in twelve-syllable (sometimes thirteen-syllable) lines, and the conclusion in thirteen-syllable lines.

Imaginary scene in a conventional "decadent" Roman setting. According to Cavafy's comment on the poem, the barbarians here are a symbol; consequently, "the emperor, the senators and the orators are not necessarily Roman."

VOICES   p. 20

First version probably written July 12, 1894, with the title "Sweet Voices."

Published December 1894.

Rewritten December 1903.

Published August 15, 1904.

In lines of 11-13-11, 13-14, 13-13-13 syllables.

LONGINGS   p. 21

Written September 1904.

Printed December (?) 1904, in Cavafy's first private collection.

In lines of fourteen syllables, rhymed *abcacb*.

TROJANS   p. 22

Written June 1900.
Published November 30, 1905.
Originally, the poem was divided into two distinct parts lettered
A (lines 1-8) and B (lines 9-21).
For other "Trojan" poems, see the note to "The Horses of Achil-
les." Priam and Hecuba were king and queen of Troy at the time of
the Trojan War.

KING DIMITRIOS   p. 23

Written August 1900.
Published June 30, 1906.
In lines of eleven and ten syllables.
Dimitrios I the Besieger (337-283 B.C.), king of Macedonia, was
deserted in 288 B.C. by his troops who, weary of fighting to increase
his power and luxury, joined the camp of his opponent, Pyrrhos,
king of Epirus. An earlier episode in his life is alluded to in "On
the March to Sinopi."

THE RETINUE OF DIONYSOS   p. 24

Written July 1903.
Published April 15, 1907.
Couplets of 12-12, 13-13, 13-13, 12-12, 12-12, 12-12, 14-14,
12-12, 12-14, 12-12, 12-12 syllables rhymed *aabbccddeeffggh-
hiijjkk*.
Cavafy is probably not describing a specific work of Hellenistic
sculpture, and Damon is certainly an imaginary character; all the
details, however, are accurate and carefully chosen. The anony-
mous king of Syracuse is probably the tyrant Hieron II, who first
assumed the royal title in 270 B.C. A talent (silver or gold) weighed
about fifty-two lbs.

MONOTONY   p. 25

Written July 1898, with the title "Like the Past."
Published February 29, 1908.
Both stanzas have the same metrical pattern: 11-15-13-15 sylla-
bles, rhymed *abab* and *cdcd*.

THE FOOTSTEPS   p. 26

First version written August 1893, with the title "The Footsteps
of the Eumenides."
Published January 26, 1897, under the heading "Ancient Days."
Rewritten December 1908.
Published September 1909.
Nero (see "Nero's Deadline") was the son of Domitius Aeno-
barbus and Agrippina Junior. She later married the emperor Clau-
dius, poisoned him, and gave the throne to her son (A.D. 54-68),
who had her murdered in A.D. 59. The *Lares familiares* were minor
Roman deities protecting the household; little statues of them were
placed by the hearth, called *Lararium*. The Furies are pursuing
Nero for his greatest crime: matricide.

THAT'S THE MAN   p. 27

Written August 1898.
Published March 1909.
The metrical pattern is 14-13-15, 12-15-15-12, 15-13-14 sylla-
bles, rhymed *abc, dccd*, and *cba*.
The title (repeated in l. 9) is a quotation from Lucian's *The
Dream*, 11, in which this hellenized Syrian sophist and writer (c.
A.D. 120-200) relates how he chose his literary career: in a dream
he saw Culture who promised him: "If ever you go abroad, even
on foreign soil you will not be unknown or inconspicuous, for I will
attach to you such marks of identification that everyone who sees

you will nudge his neighbor and point you out with his finger, saying 'That's the man!' '' (adapted from the translation by A. M. Harmon).

The scene and the anonymous protagonist of the poem are imaginary. Mesopotamian Edessa was, from 132 B.C., the capital of Osroini (see ''in a Town of Osroini''); its population was mainly Semitic. Antioch was the capital of Syria, second only to Alexandria among Cavafy's favorite ancient cities.

THE CITY   p. 28

Written August 1894, entitled ''Once More in the Same City,'' and listed under the heading ''Prisons.''

Published April 1910.

Both stanzas have an almost identical metrical pattern: 16-14-14-11-15-12 (or 10)-12-16 syllables. The rhymes, mostly homophonous, are *abbccdda* and *effggdde* (rhymes *a* and *e* are almost identical).

According to Cavafy's thematic order (see the appendix to the editor's introduction), ''The City'' and ''The Satrapy'' are the twin portals to his mature poetry at least up to 1916.

THE SATRAPY   p. 29

Perhaps first written before November 29, 1903.

Written (or rewritten) July 1905.

Published June 1910.

Only lines 4, 16, and 18 have more than the otherwise regular eleven syllables.

A satrapy was a Persian province governed by a satrap, under the ancient monarchy. In spite of the reference to king Artaxerxes (possibly the first of the three Persian monarchs of that name: 464-424 B.C.), Cavafy is reported to have said that the anonymous protagonist should not necessarily be identified with Themistokles or Dimaratos (see ''Dimaratos''), who had both been honorably received by a Persian king as political refugees, or indeed any politician, but that he symbolizes, rather, an artist or possibly a scientist. Susa was the capital of Persia under the Achaemenid dynasty (c. 645-330 B.C.).

THE IDES OF MARCH   p. 30

Written March 1906.
Published December 1910.
A soothsayer had warned Julius Caesar (see ''Theodotos'') to beware of the Ides of March, i.e., the fifteenth day of that month. On March 15, 44 B.C., the sophist Artemidoros vainly tried to hand Caesar a message disclosing the murderous plot of Brutus and Cassius.

THINGS ENDED   p. 31

Written May 1910.
Published February 1911.

SCULPTOR OF TYANA   p. 32

First written June 1893, with the title ''A Sculptor's Studio.''
Rewritten November 1903.
Published March 1911.
Rhymed *abbbc, ddaebcfe, ggbfbb*, and *gbhbh*.
The scene, set in Rome, and the anonymous protagonist are imaginary. Tyana (see ''If Actually Dead'') was a city in Cappadocia. Rhea was the daughter of Heaven and Earth, wife of Kronos, and mother of the Olympian gods. Marius (157-86 B.C.), Aemilius Paulus (228-160 B.C.), and Scipio Africanus Major (235-c.183 B.C.) or Minor (c.185-129 B.C.) were famous Roman consuls and

226

generals. For Pompey, see "Theodotos"; for Patroklos, see "The Funeral of Sarpedon" and "The Horses of Achilles"; for Kaisarion, see "Alexandrian Kings" and "Kaisarion"—therefore, Margarita Dalmati described this poem as "Cavafy's Studio."

THE GOD ABANDONS ANTONY   p. 33

Written November 1910.
Published April 1911.
The title is a quotation from Plutarch's *Life of Antony*, 75. Mark Antony believed himself to be under the special protection of the god Dionysos (see "The Retinue of Dionysos"). The poem's anonymous protagonist is not a historical figure.
For more specific historical poems concerning or mentioning Mark Antony, see "In Alexandria, 32 B.C.," "In a Township of Asia Minor," and "Antony's Ending."

IONIC   p. 34

Perhaps first written May 1886; originally entitled "Memory."
First version published October 1896.
Rewritten July 1905, with the title "Thessaly."
Final version published June 1911.

THE GLORY OF THE PTOLEMIES   p. 35

First version written August 1896.
Rewritten May 1911.
Published September 1911.
In lines of 15-14-14-15-14-14-16-12 syllables, rhymed *abbacdce* (rhymes *d* and *e* are almost homophonous).
Cavafy does not specify the identity of the Lagid (i.e., a Ptolemy, king of Egypt) or the Selefkid (i.e., king of Syria).

ITHAKA p. 36

A first, very different version, entitled "Second Odyssey," was written in January 1894 and remained unpublished until 1985.

Final version written October 1910.

Published November 1911.

The Laistrygonians and the Cyclops were cannibal giants encountered by Odysseus on his homeward journey to his native island of Ithaka.

DANGEROUS THOUGHTS p. 38

Published November 1911.

Myrtias is an imaginary character, placed by Cavafy in the joint reign of the sons of Constantine the Great (A.D. 337-350). For Konstantios II, see "Julian in Nicomedia."

PHILHELLENE p. 39

Written July 1906.

Published April 1912.

The scene and characters are imaginary. The speaker is some petty Eastern monarch who gives instructions to Sithaspis (probably a courtier) about a coin to be minted. Zagros was the name of a range of mountains dividing Media from Assyria and Susiana in Asia Minor. Phraata, a city of Media, was the winter residence of the Parthian kings.

HERODIS ATTIKOS p. 40

First version written April 1900.

Rewritten December 1911.

Published June 1912.

Herodis Attikos (c. A.D. 101-177) was a wealthy hellenized Roman politician, sophist and patron of the arts; among the splendid buildings he erected in Athens was the Odeum, still used as an open-air concert-hall and theater. Alexandros of Selefkia was nick-named "the clay Plato." According to Cavafy's judgement (re-flected in the irony of the poem), Herodis and Alexandros were un-worthy of even the slightest admiration.

This is the only mention of Athens in Cavafy's mature *corpus*.

ALEXANDRIAN KINGS   p. 41

Written May 1912.
Published July 1912.
The regal début of Cleopatra's children was stage-managed by Mark Antony (see note to "The God Abandons Antony") in 34 B.C. Alexander and Ptolemaios Philadelphos were Antony's sons, whereas Kaisarion (see "Kaisarion") was the son of Julius Caesar (see "The Ides of March" and "Theodotos"). The youngest of these so-called kings was barely two years old and Kaisarion only fourteen. Four years later Antony and Cleopatra committed suicide, Kaisarion was executed, and the younger children were taken as hostages to Rome.

COME BACK   p. 43

First version written June 1904, with the title "Sensual Mem-ory."
Rewritten September 1909.
Published October 1912.

IN CHURCH   p. 44

First version written August 1892.
Rewritten December 1901, and again May 1906.
Printed probably December 1912.
Rhymed *aaa* and *bcccdded*.

VERY SELDOM   p. 45

Written December 1911.
Published January 1913.

AS MUCH AS YOU CAN   p. 46

Written October 1905, with the title ''A Life.''
Published October 1913.

FOR THE SHOP   p. 47

Written December 1912.
Published October 1913.
Couplets of 11-11, 15-15, 15-17, 12-12, and 17-17 syllables,
rhymed *aa bb cc dd ee* (only the *e* rhymes are not homophonous).
In February 1903 Cavafy rewrote a poem, ''Artificial Flowers''
(not translated here), which remained unpublished until 1948;
though its theme is similar, it cannot be considered as an early ver-
sion of ''For the Shop.''

I WENT   p. 48

Written June 1905.
Published October 1913.

TOMB OF THE GRAMMARIAN LYSIAS   p. 49

Written February 1911.
Published March 1914.
In lines of 15-13-13-13-15-13-17-13 syllables, rhymed
abacbbcb.
Lysias the Grammarian is an imaginary character.
Between 1914 and 1918 Cavafy published five poems entitled

"Tomb of . . ." (the Grammarian Lysias, Evrion, Iasis, Ignatios, Lanis). Several other poems published by him during the same period and later (through 1928) could easily have had titles of the same type; in fact "Kimon, son of Learchos . . ." was probably first entitled "Tomb of Marikos."

TOMB OF EVRION   p. 50

Written April 1912.
Published March 1914.
Rhymed *abcaddefegcgf*.
All the persons named in this poem are imaginary, and the name of Evrion seems to be composed of the Greek word for "Jew" (Evraios) and a Greek diminutive ending. The "syenite stone" was an expensive reddish granite from Syene [= Aswan]. The Greek text states that Evrion, "on his mother's side, descended from a line of alabarchs" (i.e., magistrates of the Jewish community of Alexandria). For other Helleno-Jewish poems, see "Of the Jews," "Aristovoulos," and "Alexander Jannaios and Alexandra."

CHANDELIER   p. 51

Written April 1895.
Published June 1914.
In lines of 15-12-15-13-15 and 15-12-15-13-8 syllables, rhymed *abaac* and *dbddc*.
This symbolic poem closes Cavafy's thematic collection, *Poems: 1905-1915* (see the appendix to the editor's introduction).

LONG AGO   p. 52

Written March 1914.
Printed probably December 1914.

In lines of 10-15-15 and 12-14-14-12 syllables; only the second stanza is rhymed: *abba*.

BUT THE WISE PERCEIVE THINGS ABOUT TO HAPPEN   p. 53

First version written February 1896, with the title "Imminent Things."

Published December 1899.

Final version printed 1915, probably before June.

Both stanzas have the same metrical pattern: 12-10-13-14-10 syllables, rhymed *abcab* and *dbcdb*.

THEODOTOS   p. 54

Written before October 3, 1911, perhaps with the title "Victory."

Published June 1915.

The rhetorician Theodotos of Chios persuaded the Egyptians to kill Pompey (September 28, 48 B.C.) when he landed in Egypt as a fugitive, after his defeat by Julius Caesar (see "The Ides of March") at Pharsalus. There is no evidence that it was Theodotos who brought Caesar Pompey's head.

AT THE CAFÉ DOOR   p. 55

Perhaps written July 1904, with the title "From the Hands of Eros."

Printed 1915, probably after June.

HE SWEARS   p. 56

Written December 1905, with the title "Libidinousness."

Printed 1915, probably after June.

Each of the first four lines really consists of two lines (not hemistichs) of seven and eight syllables; the last two lines are of thirteen and eleven syllables. From 1915 to 1929 Cavafy published eighteen poems which are distinguished by the following metrical and visual peculiarity (not reproduced here): with the exception of ''He Swears,'' all are written in lines of six or seven syllables, which are printed in pairs divided by a blank space.

ONE NIGHT   p. 57

Written July 1907; first entitled ''One of my Evenings'' and then ''One of my Nights.''
Printed 1915, probably after June.

MORNING SEA   p. 58

Printed 1915, probably after June.

PICTURED   p. 59

Written August 1914.
Printed 1915, probably after June.
Rhymed *abbcadeccedb*.

OROPHERNIS   p. 60

Written February 1904.
Printed probably January 1916.
Orophernis was the supposed son of Ariarathis IV of Cappadocia. His mother was the daughter of Antiochos III the Great (see ''The Battle of Magnesia''), and his grandmother Stratoniki was the daughter of Antiochos II of Syria. A protégé of Dimitrios of Syria (see ''The Displeasure of Selefkidis'' and ''Of Dimitrios Sotir''), who assisted him in his bid for the throne of Cappadocia in 157 B.C. Three years later, Orophernis was deposed because of his rapacity,

and he fled to Antioch where he subsequently tried to usurp the throne of his protector.

THE BATTLE OF MAGNESIA   p. 62

Written November 1913.

Printed probably January 1916.

Couplets of 12-12, 16-16, 15-13, 15-15, 15-15, 14-14, 15-17, 17-17, and 17-17 syllables, rhymed *aa bb cc dd ee ff gg hh ii* (rhymes *a b c h* are homophonous).

Philip V, last king of Macedonia, had been defeated in 197 B.C. by the Romans at Cynoscephalae, partly as a result of not receiving any assistance from Antiochos III the Great, king of Syria. The imaginary scene of the poem is set seven years later, after the battle of Magnesia (see "Craftsman of Wine Bowls"), which established Roman supremacy in the Hellenized East. According to one of Cavafy's oral comments, Philip's lassitude is a sham, concealing his preparations for a new attack against the Romans.

MANUEL KOMNINOS   p. 63

Written March 1905.

Printed probably January 1916.

Lines 6-12 have eleven syllables each.

The Byzantine emperor Manuel Komninos died on September 20, 1180. He was famous as both a warrior and a lecher.

THE DISPLEASURE OF SELEFKIDIS   p. 64

Written February 1910

Printed probably January 1916.

The two protagonists of the poem are Dimitrios Selefkidis, who later ascended to the throne of Syria and adopted the title "Sotir," i.e., Savior (see "Orophernis" and "Of Dimitrios Sotir"), and

Ptolemy VI Philomitor, king of Egypt. The action takes place in 164 B.C., when Dimitrios was a hostage in Rome; Ptolemy Philomitor had been expelled from Alexandria by his own brother and co-ruler, Ptolemy VIII Evergetis (see "To Have Taken the Trouble"), and came to Rome to beg the Senate to reinstate him (see "Envoys from Alexandria").

WHEN THEY COME ALIVE   p. 66

    Written July 1913.
    Printed probably before November 1916.

IN THE STREET   p. 67

    Written July 1913.
    Printed probably December 1916.

BEFORE THE STATUE OF ENDYMION   p. 68

    Written May 1895.
    Printed probably December 1916.
    In lines of 14-12-12-14-16-12-14-16-16 syllables, rhymed *ab-babccac* (most of these rhymes are homophonous).
    The anonymous Alexandrian speaker is an imaginary character. The legendary Endymion (see "Of the Jews") was the most beautiful of mortals: Selini (i.e., the moon) fell in love with him and made Zeus preserve him in eternal sleep so she could visit him every night. One of his alleged tombs was on Mount Latmos, near Militos, in Asia Minor.

IN A TOWN OF OSROINI   p. 69

    Written August 1916, under the title "Charmidis."
    Printed 1917.

The first four lines form a regular quatrain: 15-14-14-15 sylla-
bles; the poem is rhymed *abbcdecd*.

The scene and Remon are fictitious. Osroini was a kingdom in
Mesopotamia, whose capital was Edessa (see "That's the Man").
Charmidis was Plato's uncle, killed in a political clash; he was im-
mortalized by this nephew in a dialogue bearing his name, where
Socrates, inspired by the physical perfection of young Charmidis,
seeks to define wisdom as the knowledge of good and evil. The last
two words of the poem also serve to indicate that Cavafy is not
referring to Oscar Wilde's poem entitled "Charmides" (1881).

PASSING THROUGH   p. 70

Written January 1914.
Printed 1917.
Couplets of 16-14, 16-10, 14-14, 16-14, and 12-16 syllables,
rhymed *aa bb cc dd bb* (rhymes *a* and *c* are homophonous).

FOR AMMONIS, WHO DIED AT 29, IN 610   p. 71

Written September 1915, with the title "Epitaph for the Poet
Ammonis."
Printed 1917.
Loosely rhymed *abbcd, eef, ghai* and *ajak*.
Ammonis, an Egyptian, and Raphael, a Copt, are both fictional
characters. The date coincides with the beginning of Mohammed's
career as a prophet.

ONE OF THEIR GODS   p. 72

Written June 1899, with the title "One of Them."
Printed 1917.
The scene is set in one of several Hellenistic cities called Selef-
kia, of which the most splendid by far was Selefkia on Tigris,

founded c. 312 B.C. by Selefkos I Nicator as the capital of his empire.

IN THE EVENING   p. 73

Written March 1916, with the title "Alexandrian."
Printed 1917.
Rhymed *abacadd, efaag*, and *bhij*. The first *a* rhyme of the first stanza and the two *a* rhymes of the second are homophonous, as are the second and third *a* rhymes of the first stanza.

TO SENSUAL PLEASURE   p. 74

Written September 1913.
Printed 1917.
In lines of 14-16-16-13 syllables.
In the original, the title consists of a single word in the dative form commonly used for dedications.
This is the shortest of Cavafy's published poems.

GRAY   p. 75

Written February 1917.
Published May 1917.
In the original, the sex of the person with the gray eyes remains ambiguous.

TOMB OF IASIS   p. 76

Written April 1917.
Published May 1917.
In lines of 17-12-17-12 and 18-15-16-15 syllables, rhymed *abab* and *cdcd* (rhymes *a* and *c* are homophonous).
Iasis is an imaginary character.
Narcissus was a minor mythological figure, the beautiful but dis-

dainful son of the river-god Kiphissos. The nymph Echo fell desperately in love with him, and Aphrodite punished him by causing him to waste away for love of his own watery reflection. The gods transformed him into the flower that bears his name. For Hermes as an object of sexual desire, see "Sculptor of Tyana."

IN THE MONTH OF ATHYR   p. 77

Written March 1917.
Published May 1917.
Each line really consists of two lines of either six or seven syllables, sporadically rhymed.
In the Egyptian calendar, the month of Athyr (the goddess of tombs and carnal love) corresponded to October-November. The "Kappa Zeta" (KZ) is the number twenty-seven in Greek numerals. The inscription and Lefkios are imaginary.

I'VE LOOKED SO MUCH. . . .   p. 78

Written October 1911, with the title "For the Beautiful Things."
Published May 1917.
Sporadically rhymed.

TOMB OF IGNATIOS   p. 79

Written April 1916, with the title "Tomb of Hieronymos."
Printed 1917.
Kleon-Ignatios is an imaginary character; the change of his "worldly" name is in accordance with regular monastic practice.

DAYS OF 1903   p. 80

Written March 1909, with the title "March 1907."
Printed 1917.
Cavafy published five poems entitled "Days of . . ." (1896,

1901, 1903, 1908, and 1909, '10, and '11). Though obviously related to his "secret life," their dates are mostly useless for biographical purposes (see the note to "Days of 1901"). In 1903, Cavafy turned 40; there is further evidence that this was a year of particular importance to him (cf. under "Unpublished Poems" those entitled "September 1903" and "December 1903").

This poem closes Cavafy's thematic collection, *Poems: 1916-1918* (see the appendix to the editor's introduction).

THE WINDOW OF THE TOBACCO SHOP   p. 81

Written September 1907, with the title "The Closed Carriage."
Printed 1917.

KAISARION   p. 82

Written December 1914, with the title "Of Ptolemy Caesar."
Printed 1918.
The first stanza is rhymed *ababcaadee*.
Kaisarion, i.e., "Little Caesar," or Ptolemy XVI, was the son of Julius Caesar and was Cleopatra's eldest child. In 34 B.C., Mark Antony conferred on him the title "King of Kings" (see "Alexandrian Kings"). After Antony's defeat (see "The God Abandons Antony," "In Alexandria, 31 B.C."), his victorious opponent, Gaius Julius Caesar Octavianus (i.e., the future emperor Augustus), who was Caesar's adopted son, ordered the execution of Kaisarion. This execution was the practical result of political advice paraphrasing an expression from the *Iliad* (II, 204): "It is not a good thing to have many Caesars . . ."

BODY, REMEMBER. . . .   p. 84

Written May 1916.
Published December 1917 or January 1918.

TOMB OF LANIS   p. 85

Written December 1916.
Published December 1917 or January 1918.
In fifteen-syllable lines.
All the characters are imaginary: Lanis is a Greek name; Rame-
tichos, Egyptian; and Marcus, Roman. The anonymous painter is
called Kyrenian, i.e., a native of Cyrene (see "Kimon, Son of Lear-
chos . . ."), an important center of commerce and Greek culture in
Libya. Hyacinthus is a minor mythological figure, a mortal young
man loved by Apollo and killed by jealous Zephyr; from his blood
sprang the flower that bears his name.

UNDERSTANDING   p. 86

Written February 1915.
Published December 1917 or January 1918.

NERO'S DEADLINE   p. 87

Written December 1915, with the title "Towards the Fall."
Published May 1918.
In the spring of A.D. 68, Servius Sulpicius Galba (c. 3-69), then
Roman governor of Eastern Spain, was invited by the army to re-
place the emperor Nero (see "The Footsteps"), who committed sui-
cide shortly thereafter. Nero's visit to Achaia (i.e., Greece), during
which he consulted the oracle, took place one year earlier.

ENVOYS FROM ALEXANDRIA   p. 88

Written June 1915.
Printed 1918.
Couplets forming two stanzas of 16-16-17-17-16-16-12-14 and

14-14-14-12-13-17-14-16 syllables, rhymed *aabbccdd* and *eeffgghh*; rhymes *a* and *b* are homophonous, and rhymes *f* and *h* almost identical with rhyme *d*.

The scene is probably invented, but the "rival Ptolemaic kings" are Ptolemy VI Philomitor (see "The Displeasure of Selefkidis"), and Ptolemy VIII Evergetis (i.e., Benefactor, commonly known as Kakergetis, i.e., Malefactor: see "To Have Taken the Trouble"), co-rulers of Egypt from 170 to 164 B.C. Philomitor was restored alone to the throne by the Romans in 157 B.C.

ARISTOVOULOS   p. 89

Written October 1916.
Published July 1918.
In order to exclude completely the Asmonaean dynasty (i.e., the Maccabees: see "Alexander Jannaios and Alexandra") from the throne of Judaea, Herod I the Great (73-4 B.C.), at the instigation of his mother Kypros and his sister Salome, in 35 B.C. ordered the drowning of Aristovoulos, brother of his own wife Mariamme and son of his mother-in-law Alexandra. A few months earlier, Aristovoulos, whose beauty had stirred the interest of Antony (cf. "Alexandria Kings"), had been named high priest by Herod, though he was barely seventeen.

IN THE HARBOR-TOWN   p. 91

Written September 1917, with the title "Tomb of Doros."
Published July 1918.
Mostly couplets in lines of 13-13-15-11-15-15-14-12-15-8-9-14 syllables, rhymed *aabbccddaeae*.
Emis is an imaginary character.

AIMILIANOS MONAI, ALEXANDRIAN, A.D. 628-655   p. 92

Probably first written November 1898, with the title "Protected." That early version may have consisted of only the first two stanzas.

Printed 1918.

The metrical pattern of the first two stanzas is 13-11-13-13 syllables, and of the third 15-14-14-14 syllables, rhymed *abab, cdcd,* and *effg*.

Aimilianos Monai is an imaginary character; the dates of the title suggest that, in his early youth, he had to abandon Alexandria because of its conquest by the Moslems (A.D. 641).

This is the earliest of Cavafy's six published poems embedding another poem of his (see "Imenos," "If Actually Dead," "Those who Fought for the Achaian League," "Epitaph of Antiochos . . . ," "Kimon, Son of Learchos . . ."). In 1891, Cavafy wrote a different example of this technique, "Correspondence after Baudelaire," a poem of thirty-seven lines incorporating his own translation of Baudelaire's famous sonnet "Correspondances," which remained unpublished until 1966.

SINCE NINE O'CLOCK   p. 93

Written November 1917, with the title "Half Past Twelve."
Printed 1918.

For the last twenty-five years of his life, Cavafy lived alone in Alexandria in the famous apartment on Rue Lepsius. His reference to "family grief" includes the deaths of his father (1870) and mother (1899), and of his brothers Peter (1891), George (1900), Aristeidis (1902), and Alexander (1905).

According to Cavafy's thematic order (see the appendix to the editor's introduction), this poem was placed at the beginning of the booklet *Poems, 1916-1918*.

OUTSIDE THE HOUSE   p. 94

Written July 1917.
Printed probably January 1919.

THE NEXT TABLE   p. 95

Written January 1918.
Printed probably January 1919.
A casino, in those days, was a respectable public establishment
for entertainment, including gambling.
In the original, the sex of the person sitting at the next table re-
mains ambiguous.

THE AFTERNOON SUN   p. 96

Written November 1918.
Printed 1919.
Loosely rhymed.
In the original, the sex of the former tenant of the room remains
ambiguous.

COMES TO REST   p. 97

Written March 1918.
Printed July 1919.

OF THE JEWS (A.D. 50)   p. 98

Written October 1912.
Printed probably before June 1919.
Ianthis, son of Antony, is a fictional character. Though a Jew, his
name is Greek and his father's name Roman. The date of the title
places him near the end of the reign of Claudius (A.D. 41-54), who

restored the privileges of the Alexandrian Jews, though without granting them rights equal to those enjoyed by the Greeks. For Endymion, see "Before the Statue of Endymion."

IMENOS p. 99

The first version (without the historical background of the second stanza) was written October 1915, with the title "Love It the More," and remained unpublished until 1968.
Rewritten February 1919.
Printed 1919.
Imenos is an imaginary character, placed by Cavafy in the reign of the young and able Byzantine emperor Michael III (842-867), nicknamed "The Drunkard" by the apologists of his murderous co-emperor Basil I. The letter quoted is fictional.

ON BOARD SHIP p. 100

Written October 1919, with the title "The Ionian Sea."
Printed December 1919.
Cavafy had sailed through the Ionian Sea in July-August 1901.

OF DIMITRIOS SOTIR (162-150 B.C.) p. 101

Written March 1915.
Printed September 1919.
Grandson of Antiochos III the Great, who had been defeated by the Romans at Lydian Magnesia in 190 B.C. (see "The Battle of Magnesia" and "Craftsman of Wine Bowls"), and son of Selefkos IV, Dimitrios spent his youth in Rome (see "The Displeasure of Selefkidis") as a hostage; meanwhile the throne of Syria was being usurped first by his uncle, Antiochos IV Epiphanis (see "To Antiochos Epiphanis" and "Temethos, Antiochian, A.D. 400"), and later by his cousin, Antiochos V. In 162 B.C. Dimitrios escaped

from Italy, recovered his throne, and struggled to restore the unity and leadership of Syria. His abilities caused him to be feared by his neighbors and to be suspect to Rome; he made enemies even among those he had protected (see "Orophernis"), became morose, and took to drink. In 150 B.C. he was defeated and killed by a pretender to the throne, the adventurer Alexander Valas (see "The Favor of Alexander Valas") who had been suborned by the former satrap of Babylon, Herakleidis (see "Craftsman of Wine Bowls"), Attalos II of Pergamos, and Ptolemy VI Philomitor (see "The Displeasure of Selefkidis" and "Envoys from Alexandria").

IF ACTUALLY DEAD   p. 103

The first version, written October 1897, with the title "Absence," consisted of the first part only; it remained unpublished until 1984.

Rewritten July 1910 and March 1920.

Printed March 1920.

The title is a quotation from Flavius Philostratos' *Life of Apollonios of Tyana*, VIII, 29, a "biography" written c. A.D. 200, which Cavafy greatly admired. The philosopher and magus Apollonios (c. 4 B.C.-A.D. 96 or 98) was born in Tyana (see "Sculptor of Tyana"). After studying Greek philosophy and adopting the ascetic life of a strict Pythagorean, he travelled widely in the East (even visiting India) and became famous for his miraculous powers. The last years of his life were spent in Ephesos, though one legend had it that he "disappeared" at the temple of Athena at Lindos (in Rhodes), and another placed his "assumption" at the temple of Diktynna (i.e., Britomartis, a Minoan goddess) in Crete. Many of his wonders, which are related by Philostratos, have clear similarities to the miracles of Christ—indeed, some have seen the *Life* as a kind of anti-Gospel. Philostratos' biography was allegedly based on the memoirs of Damis, one of Apollonios' pupils.

The second part of the poem attributes the fictional monologue of the first to an imaginary Alexandrian pagan, living in the reign of the emperor Justin I the Elder (518-527), an uncouth soldier who was the uncle of Justinian

Cavafy used Philostratos' text in two other of his published poems (see "But the Wise Perceive Things About to Happen" and "Apollonios of Tyana in Rhodes"); a third poem, entitled "Athanasios," remained unfinished and was first published in 1981.

YOUNG MEN OF SIDON (A.D. 400)   p. 105

Written June 1920.
Printed June 1920.
Rhymed *ab, cdbd, eefdghi,* and *jkllmjnhjknhm.*
The date of the title (see also "Theatre of Sidon . . ." and "Temethos, Antiochian . . .") probably suggests the imminent irruption of the barbarians into the scene of the ancient world (see "Waiting for the Barbarians"). Sidon (see "Theatre of Sidon") was a prosperous hellenized city on the coast of Phoenicia; it started declining after A.D. 20 and was conquered by the Arabs in 637/8. The anonymous characters are imaginary.

Meleager (fl. c. 100 B.C.), Krinagoras (first c. B.C.), and Rhianos (b. 275 B.C.) were minor Hellenistic poets. The epigram referred to and quoted in the third stanza is said to have been written by Aeschylus (525-456 B.C.) himself as his own epitaph. The complete text, in translation, reads as follows: "In this tomb lies Aeschylus, son of Euphorion, an Athenian, who died in wheat-bearing Gela [in Sicily]. The Marathonian grove could proclaim his tested valor, as well as the long-haired Persian who tried it." Datis and Artaphernis were the leaders of the Persian punitive expedition which ended at the battle of Marathon (490 B.C.), where the Athenians—among them Aeschylus—defeated the invaders.

Of the three major Athenian tragedians, Aeschylus seems to have been Cavafy's favorite, though this may not be clearly evident from the *corpus* of the "Published Poems" (see the note to "Walls" and the epigraph to "Unfaithfulness"). One of the early published and later rejected poems ("The Vote of Athena," 1892/94) and two of the "Unpublished Poems" ("The Naval Battle," 1899—not translated in this volume—and "When the Watchman Saw the Light," 1900) are directly inspired by Aeschylean tragedies.

TO CALL UP THE SHADES   p. 106

Printed August 1920.

Each line really consists of two lines of either six or seven syllables, rhymed *abcded* and *afghgijbed*.

For a more concrete example of Cavafy's poetic necromancy, see "Kaisarion."

DAREIOS   p. 107

Written May 1917, but possibly first written before 1897.

Printed October 1920.

The scene and the timorous poet Phernazis (a Persian name), both fictitious, are probably set in 74 B.C., in the strategically and commercially important city of Amisos, on the coast of Pontos (Black Sea), which fell to the Romans in 71 B.C.

Dareios I (521-486 B.C.) was, after Cyrus the Great (559-529 B.C.), the greatest of the Achaemenid kings of Persia; in European history he is chiefly known for the defeat of his invading force at Marathon in 490 B.C. (see "Young Men of Sidon" and "Dimaratos"). The actual circumstances of his rise to the throne of Persia are obscure and suspicious; therefore Phernazis, for their poetic treatment, faces a choice between historical truth, courtly caution, and psychological plausibility.

Mithridatis VI Evpator (= "The Good Father") was the semi-hellenized Persian king of Pontos (120-63 B.C.). Cicero designated him the greatest of all rulers after Alexander and the most formidable opponent of Rome in the East. He ascended to the throne in c. 115 B.C., jointly with his brother, whom he subsequently killed. In 74 B.C., he launched the Third Mithridatic War against the numerically inferior Romans in Bithynia. Defeated by Lucullus and Pompey (see "Theodotos") in 66 B.C., he was overthrown by his own son, Pharnacis, who drove him to suicide.

ANNA KOMNINA   p. 109

Written August 1917.
Printed December 1920.
The first two lines, each of twelve syllables, are rhymed.
Anna Komnina (1083-1153/4) was the first-born daughter of the Byzantine emperor Alexios I Komninos (see "Anna Dalassini"). In 1118, she vainly tried to usurp the succession to the throne from her brother, John II, on behalf of her husband, Nikiphoros Vryennios, whose death (1136/7) deprived her of every worldly hope. She retired to a monastery and wrote the *Alexiad*, a biography of her father, from which the quotations of the second stanza are drawn.

A BYZANTINE NOBLEMAN IN EXILE COMPOSING VERSES   p. 110

Written March 1921.
Printed March 1921.
Sporadically rhymed.
The anonymous protagonist is a fictitious character, perhaps modelled on (but not identifiable with) the Byzantine emperor Michael VII, dethroned in 1078 by Nikiphoros III Botaniatis, who was himself dethroned in 1081 by Alexios I Komninos (see the note to "Anna Komnina"), husband of Irini Doukaina (1066-1123).

THEIR BEGINNING   p. 111

Written June 1915.
Printed March 1921.

THE FAVOR OF ALEXANDER VALAS   p. 112

Probably written June 1916, with the title "The Wheel of the
Chariot."
Printed June 1921.
Lines of 13-13-13-15-10-14-16-17-15 syllables, rhymed
ababcccd (rhymes *a* and *b* are homophonous).
The anonymous protagonist and the circumstances are probably
fictitious. Valas, king of Syria (150-145 B.C.), is the impostor men-
tioned in "Of Dimitrios Sotir."

MELANCHOLY OF JASON KLEANDER, POET IN KOMMAGINI,
A.D. 595   p. 113

Probably written August 1918, with the title "Knife."
Printed June 1921.
Jason is an imaginary character. Kommagini (see "Epitaph of
Antiochos, King of Kommagini"), once a small independent state
northeast of Syria (164 B.C.-A.D. 72), was part of the Byzantine
Empire until 638, when it was conquered by the Arabs. The date of
the title places Jason's monologue fifty-three years after the plun-
dering of Kommagini by Hosroes I of Persia, and four years after
the peace treaty signed by the Byzantine emperor Mavrikios and
Hosroes II.

DIMARATOS   p. 114

First written August 1904.
Rewritten November 1911.
Printed September 1921.

The mention of Porphyry (one of the chief exponents of Neoplatonism and a pupil of Plotinus) places the composition of this imaginary sophistic essay between 263 and 305 B.C., in Sicily or Rome. The situation described in the essay is set in Persia c. 480 B.C. Dimaratos was king of Sparta from 510 to 491 B.C.; his scheming fellow-king, Kleomenis I, aided by Leotychidis (who succeeded Dimaratos), bribed the Delphic Oracle to establish that Dimaratos was not a genuine son of King Ariston. Dimaratos took refuge at the court of Dareios I (see "Dareios"), where he was welcomed as an expert in Greek affairs. He subsequently accompanied Xerxes on his disastrous campaign against the Greeks, at the end of which Leotychidis played a decisive role as commander-in-chief of the Greek fleet.

I'VE BROUGHT TO ART   p. 116

Written September 1921.
Printed September 1921.
Each line really consists of two lines of either six or seven syllables.

FROM THE SCHOOL OF THE RENOWNED PHILOSOPHER   p. 117

Written December 1921.
Printed December 1921.
The anonymous protagonist is imaginary. The poem is set shortly before the death of Ammonios Sakkas (A.D. 243), the "Socrates of Neoplatonism," who taught in Alexandria and was said to have had Plotinus and the philosopher Origen among his disciples.

CRAFTSMAN OF WINE BOWLS   p. 119

First written November 1903, with the title "The Amphora."
Rewritten July 1912 and December 1921.
Printed December 1921.

Each line really consists of two lines of either six or seven syllables, sporadically rhymed.

The anonymous protagonist and the situation are imaginary. The battle of Magnesia (see ''The Battle of Magnesia'' and ''Of Dimitrios Sotir'') took place in 190 B.C.; the monologue, therefore, is set in c. 175 B.C., when Herakleidis was the treasurer of Antiochos IV Epiphanis (see ''To Antiochos Epiphanis'' and ''Temethos, Antiochian, A.D. 400'').

THOSE WHO FOUGHT FOR THE ACHAIAN LEAGUE   p. 120

Written February 1922.
Printed February 1922.
The epigram forming the first part of the poem is ascribed to an anonymous, imaginary Greek, writing in 110/9 B.C. about historical events of 146 B.C. The Achaian League (280-146 B.C.) was the last attempt of the mainland Greeks to maintain their independence; it was dissolved in 146, when its unworthy generals, Diaios and Kritolaos, were crushed by the Romans at Skarfeia in the Locris and at Lefkopetra in Corinth (see ''On an Italian Shore''). Ptolemy IX, nicknamed ''Lathyros'' (= Chick-pea), was an equally unworthy ruler; he reigned intermittently from 116 to 80 B.C.

Since 1926, this poem has been read by several friends of Cavafy as alluding to the Asia Minor disaster of 1922.

TO ANTIOCHOS EPIPHANIS   p. 121

First written probably November 1911, with the title of ''Antiochos Epiphanis.''
Final version written February 1922.
Printed February 1922.
Each line really consists of two lines of either six or seven syllables, sporadically rhymed.

The scene, and the anonymous young protégé of Antiochos IV Epiphanis (175-163 B.C.—see "Temethos, Antiochian, A.D. 400"), are imaginary but can be dated to 169/8 B.C. The king's father was Antiochos III the Great (223-187 B.C.), who had been decisively defeated by the Romans in 190 B.C. at the battle of Magnesia (see "Of Dimitrios Sotir" and "The Battle of Magnesia"). Epiphanis' brother was Selefkos IV Philopator, who was murdered in 175 B.C. and whose daughter married Perseus, last king of Macedonia. The new attempt of the Macedonians (who had already been beaten by the Romans in 197 B.C.) to retain their independence, resulted in the total defeat of Perseus at the battle of Pydna (168 B.C.). Tyre was a prosperous city on the shores of Phoenicia and the center for the commerce in purple dye.

IN AN OLD BOOK   p. 122

Perhaps first written in September 1892, with the title "The Book."
Printed December 1922.

IN DESPAIR   p. 123

Written May 1923.
Printed May 1923.
Each line really consists of two lines of either six or seven syllables, loosely rhymed. In the Greek text of this poem, the effect, according to Seferis, is that of a popular tango.

JULIAN SEEING CONTEMPT   p. 124

Written September (?) 1923.
Printed September 4, 1923.
Rhymed *abbcdbcefdcg*.

From 1896 to 1932/3 Cavafy wrote at least seven poems directed against the Roman emperor Julian (A.D. 361-363): "Julian at the Mysteries," "Julian Seeing Contempt," "Julian in Nicomedia," "A Great Procession of Priests and Laymen," "Julian and the Antiochians," "You Didn't Understand," "On the Outskirts of Antioch." The first remained unpublished until 1968.

Julian was dubbed "The Apostate" because, though originally a Christian, he tried unsuccessfully to revive paganism as an austere religion based upon Neoplatonism and organized along more puritanical lines than prevailed in the early Christian Church. The quotation in the poem is from a letter of his, written in January 363, appointing Theodoros High Priest throughout Asia. This letter elaborates the views expressed in an earlier letter to the High Priest of Gaul, Arsacius.

The last line of the poem quotes an ancient Greek maxim: *"Meden agan"* ("Nothing in excess"), attributed to one of the legendary "Seven Sages," the Spartan Chilon (fl. 536 B.C.).

EPITAPH OF ANTIOCHOS, KING OF KOMMAGINI   p. 125

Written November (?) 1923.

Printed November 2, 1923.

Rhymed *abcddededf* and *ccgcghh*.

The epitaph quoted and the characters mentioned in this poem are imaginary. If Cavafy had specifically in mind one of several homonymous kings who reigned in Kommagini (see "The Melancholy of Jason Kleander") between 64 B.C. and A.D. 72, a likely candidate is Antiochos I (c. 69-30 B.C.) who was variously known as The Just, The Friend of Rome, and The Philhellene. As in "But the Wise Perceive Things About to Happen," Cavafy suggests here a treble hierarchy: gods, Hellenic men, barbarians.

THEATRE OF SIDON (A.D. 400)   p. 126

Written November (?) 1923.
Printed November 2, 1923.
Each line really consists of two lines of either six or seven sylla-
bles, sporadically rhymed.
For Sidon and the date of the title, see the note to "Young Men
of Sidon (A.D. 400)." The "puritans who prattle about morals" are
the Christians. The anonymous speaker is an imaginary character.

JULIAN IN NICOMEDIA   p. 127

Written January 1924 (?).
Printed January 3, 1924.
Couplets of 11-13, 12-14, 13-17, 17-15, 14-16, 13-13, 11-13,
and 11-15 syllables, rhymed *aa bb cc dd ee ff gg hh*.
The scene is set in Nicomedia, a port city and capital of Bithynia,
in A.D. 351/2, when Julian (see the note to "Julian Seeing Con-
tempt") was twenty years old and had started flirting with pagan-
ism. Chrysanthios was a Neoplatonic philosopher and a friend of
Maximos of Ephesos. The latter had initiated Julian into the theur-
gic (i.e., magic) rites. Gallus was Julian's elder half-brother; he was
proclaimed caesar in 350 by their cousin, the Christian emperor
Konstantios II (see "Dangerous Thoughts"), but was executed on
the emperor's orders in 354. Julian was named as his successor, and
in 360 he was proclaimed emperor by his army, but did not ascend
to the throne until 361. Mardonios, a eunuch of Scythian or Gothic
origin, was Julian's Hellenophile tutor.

BEFORE TIME ALTERED THEM   p. 128

Written January 1924 (?).
Printed January 3, 1924.

Each lines really consists of two lines of either six or seven syllables, sporadically rhymed.

HE HAD COME THERE TO READ   p. 129

Written July (?) 1924.
Printed July 7, 1924.
Loosely rhymed *ababcdefddg*.

IN ALEXANDRIA, 31 B.C.   p. 130

First written April 1917.
Rewritten July (?) 1924.
Printed July 7, 1924.
Couplets of 15-13, 15-13, 14-16, 12-16, and 14-14 syllables, rhymed *aa aa bb cc cc* (the *a* rhymes are homophonous).

The anonymous protagonist and the incident described in this poem are imaginary. In September 31 B.C., Antony (see "Antony's Ending" and "The God Abandons Antony") and Cleopatra (see "Alexandrian Kings") were finally defeated by Octavius in the sea-battle of Actium (see "In a Township of Asia Minor"). Cleopatra tried to conceal the defeat from her subjects and staged a triumphal return to Alexandria.

JOHN KANTAKUZINOS TRIUMPHS   p. 131

Printed December 9, 1924.
Rhymed *abcc b dedf gffhhiij kllffmm* (the *j* and *k* rhymes are almost identical).

The anonymous, fictional protagonist is set in the year 1347. When the Byzantine emperor Andronikos III Palaiologos died (1341), John Kantakuzinos, a wealthy favorite of his, was appointed Regent. This led to an open clash between him and the widow of Andronikos, Anna of Savoy, mother of the eleven-year-old heir to the throne, John V. Although of French origin, Anna was supported by the Patriarch of Constantinople. In 1347, Kantakuzinos, assisted by rich landowners of Thrace and Thessaly, "triumphed" in this struggle. He was crowned joint-emperor with his wife, Irini Assan (see "Of Colored Glass"), granddaughter of the tsar of Bulgaria, John III.

TEMETHOS, ANTIOCHIAN, A.D. 400   p. 132

Printed January 20, 1925.

Each line really consists of two lines of either six or seven syllables, with occasional rhymes.

Cavafy's Temethos and Temethos' Emonidis are both imaginary characters. On the year A.D. 400, see "Young Men of Sidon" and cf. "Theatre of Sidon." On Antiochos IV Epiphanis (175-164 B.C.), see "To Antiochos Epiphanis." Samosata was the capital of Kommagini (see "The Melancholy of Jason Kleander" and "Epitaph of Antiochos, King of Kommagini"). The "137th year of the Greek kingdom" is 175 B.C., counted from the founding of the Selefkid dynasty by Selefkos I Nikator (312-281 B.C.): cf. *Macc.*, I, 10.

OF COLORED GLASS   p. 133

Printed February 27, 1925.

The coronation ceremony of John Kantakuzinos and Irini Assan (see "John Kantakuzinos Triumphs") took place in the church of the palace of Vlachernai because the cathedral of St. Sophia was partly ruined at the time. Anna of Savoy, in her struggle against Kantakuzinos, had exhausted the finances of the empire and pawned even the jewels of the crown.

THE TWENTY-FIFTH YEAR OF HIS LIFE   p. 134

Probably written June 1918, with the title "The 23rd year of my life, in the winter."
Printed June 30, 1925.

ON AN ITALIAN SHORE   p. 135

Printed June 30, 1925.
Each line really consists of two lines of either six or seven syllables, sporadically rhymed. Nearly all the rhymes are homophonous.
The protagonist and the scene are imaginary. The date is 146 B.C., when the Roman consul Lucius Mummius, after destroying the Achaean League at Lefkopetra (see "Those who Fought for the Achaian League"), sacked Corinth—killing all the men, selling the women and children into slavery, and razing all the houses—and shipped all its art treasures to Italy.

IN THE BORING VILLAGE   p. 136

Written in 1925.
Printed October 20, 1925.
Rhymed *abcdeffcfcghi*. The first two *c* rhymes are identical and the third homophonous.
The village referred to is an Egyptian village in the early twentieth century and the shop presumably that of a cotton merchant. The city, therefore, must be either Cairo or Alexandria.

APOLLONIOS OF TYANA IN RHODES   p. 137

Written in 1925.
Printed October 20, 1925.
Rhymed *abaccdef* and *daf* (the *f* rhymes are identical).

For Apollonios, see "If Actually Dead." The quotation is from Philostratos' *Life of Apollonios*, V, 22.

KLEITOS' ILLNESS   p. 138

Printed February 10, 1926.
Loosely rhymed *aabcd, cce, f*, and *gfhijkeelec*. The last three *e* rhymes are homophonous.
The characters and the scene are imaginary; the time, perhaps the middle of the fourth century A.D. (cf. "Myris . . .").

IN A TOWNSHIP OF ASIA MINOR   p. 139

Printed March 30, 1926.
The scene and the decree, both imaginary, are set in 31 B.C. (see the note to "In Alexandria, 31 B.C."). Cf. also "From the School of the Renowned Philosopher" and "When the Watchman Saw the Light."

PRIEST AT THE SERAPEION   p. 140

Printed June 9, 1926.
The anonymous protagonists are fictional. The Serapeion was the famous temple of Serapis (or Sarapis) in Alexandria (see "Myris . . ."), first built by Ptolemy I Sotir c. 300 B.C., then splendidly rebuilt by Ptolemy III Evergetes (246-221 B.C.; see "In Sparta") and destroyed by the emperor Theodosius in A.D. 391. Serapis was not one of the ancient Egyptian gods, but a syncretic combination of Osiris and Apis, with elements of Zeus, Dionysus, Pluto, and Asclepius. His official worship as patron of Alexandria was promoted by the Ptolemies, and his priests were mostly Greeks.

IN THE TAVERNAS   p. 141

Printed June 9, 1926.

Each line really consists of two lines of either six or seven sylla-
bles, sporadically rhymed.

The characters are imaginary.

A GREAT PROCESSION OF PRIESTS AND LAYMEN   p. 142

First version probably written September 1892, with the title
"The Cross."

Rewritten probably March 1917.

Printed August 30, 1926.

Sporadically rhymed.

On June 26, 363, the emperor Julian (see the note to "Julian
Seeing Contempt") was killed fighting against the Persians. His
successor, Jovian, a tolerant Christian army commander, reigned
for only seven months. The procession takes place on Holy Cross
Day, i.e., September 14, 363.

SOPHIST LEAVING SYRIA   p. 143

Printed November 15, 1926.

Each line really consists of two lines of either six or seven sylla-
bles, sporadically rhymed.

The protagonists are fictitious. Cavafy had used the name of
Mevis in a very different poem (see "Simeon") which remained
unpublished until 1968. A gold stater was approximately equivalent
to a gold sovereign.

JULIAN AND THE ANTIOCHIANS   p. 144

Printed November 15, 1926.

The epigraph is from a satirical work by the emperor Julian (see the note to "Julian Seeing Contempt") in which he attacks the people of Antioch, then a Christian city, for their hostile attitude toward his futile attempts to restore paganism in his own prudish and aristocratic form. His short residence in Antioch (361-362; see also "On the Outskirts of Antioch") also showed the inadequacy of his economic and social policy. Concerning Julian's "childish fear of the theatre," we have his own testimony that he first went to the theatre when his beard had more hair than his head; as for his "ridiculous [i.e. philosopher's] beard," he stated that he let it grow to punish his face, which nature had made ugly.

ANNA DALASSINI   p. 145

Printed January 4, 1927.
Rhymed *aabcddbc*.
In 1081, when setting off to war, the Byzantine emperor Alexis I Komninos (1081-1118) officially entrusted his mother, Anna Dalassini, with all the other affairs of state. The "golden bull" (i.e., the imperial decree) appointing her Regent of the Empire is quoted by his daughter Anna Komnina (see "Anna Komnina") in her *Alexiad*, III, 6.

DAYS OF 1896   p. 146

Written 1925.
Printed March 26, 1927.
Each line really consists of two lines of either six or seven syllables, sporadically rhymed.
See the note to "Days of 1903."

TWO YOUNG MEN, 23 TO 24 YEARS OLD   p. 147

Printed June 14, 1927.

GREEK FROM ANCIENT TIMES   p. 149

Printed September 9, 1927.

Each line really consists of two lines of either six or seven sylla-
bles, sporadically rhymed.

According to one tradition, Io, daughter of the king of Argos,
Inachos, was changed into a heifer by Zeus and chased by Hera into
Syria, where she died. In her honor, Argive colonists built a temple
and a town, and on the same site Selefkos I Nikator founded the
capital of Syria (300 B.C.).

DAYS OF 1901   p. 150

Written before October 15, 1927, first with the title "Days of
1900" and then (provisionally) "Days of 1898"; the latter title was
finally given to a poem published in 1932!

Printed October 28, 1927.

See the note to "Days of 1903."

YOU DIDN'T UNDERSTAND   p. 151

Printed January 16, 1928.

The poem is based on an untranslatable piece of wordplay (*aneg-
non, egnon, kategnon*) quoted in Sozomenos' *Ecclesiastical His-
tory*, V, 18, and addressed by the emperor Julian (see the note to
"Julian Seeing Contempt") to the Christians to deride their adap-
tations of the Greek classics or the Homeric version of the Psalms
composed by the bishop of Laodicea, Apollinaris. The Christians'
response (also quoted by Sozomenos) shows them to have been just
as skilled as Julian in the art of rhetorical sophistry.

Ever since its first publication, this poem was considered to be a
veiled reply to the critical reservations expressed by the well-known
Alexandrian critic Timos Malanos.

A YOUNG POET IN HIS TWENTY-FOURTH YEAR   p. 152

Printed January 16, 1928.

IN SPARTA   p. 153

Printed April 17, 1928.
Sporadically rhymed.
The king of Sparta, Kleomenis III (236-222 B.C.), in his desper-
ate attempt to reform the antiquated constitution of the legendary
Lykurgus which had depleted the military power of Sparta, had
asked Ptolemy III to help him fight the Macedonians and the
Achaean League. Ptolemy agreed on condition that Kleomenis'
own mother, Kratisiklia (see "Come, O King of the Lacedaimoni-
ans"), and his children, be sent to Alexandria as hostages. Com-
pared to the kings of Sparta, who claimed to be descended from
Heracles, the Ptolemies (whose dynasty dated from 304 B.C.) were
mere upstarts. Cf. "The Glory of the Ptolemies."

PICTURE OF A 23-YEAR-OLD PAINTED BY HIS FRIEND
OF THE SAME AGE, AN AMATEUR   p. 154

Printed April 17, 1928.
Each line really consists of two lines of either six or seven sylla-
bles, sometimes rhymed.

IN A LARGE GREEK COLONY, 200 B.C.   p. 155

Printed April 17, 1928.
Loosely rhymed *aabbc, aaddceef, ghfgccchh, iif, abajc,* and
bakakb.
The date (see "In the Year 200 B.C.") places this geographically
undetermined Greek colony at the hinge of the Hellenistic period:
three years before the battle of Cynoscephalae, where Philip V of

Macedonia (see the note to ''The Battle of Magnesia'') was crushingly defeated by the Romans, and ten years before the battle of Magnesia.

A PRINCE FROM WESTERN LIBYA   p. 157

Printed August 20, 1928.

Sporadically rhymed.

The protagonist and the situation are imaginary but by no means untypical (cf. ''Going Back Home from Greece''). Libya was the Greek name for Africa in general.

KIMON, SON OF LEARCHOS, 22, STUDENT OF GREEK
LITERATURE (IN KYRINI)   p. 158

Perhaps first written December 1913, with the title ''Tomb of Marikos.''

Printed August 20, 1928.

Each line really consists of two lines of either six or seven syllables, sporadically rhymed.

The protagonists and the epitaph are imaginary. Marylos is the Hellenized form of the Latin name Marullus. Kyrini was a commercial and intellectual center in present-day Libya and the birthplace of the philosopher Aristippos, a pupil of Socrates, and the poet Callimachos (c. 305-c. 240 B.C.).

ON THE MARCH TO SINOPI   p. 160

Printed December 6, 1928.

The protagonist is Mithridatis V Evergetis, king of Pontos and father of Mithridatis VI Evpator (see ''Dareios''). He was murdered in 120 B.C. in his capital, Sinopi, by his wife, who disagreed with his expansionist and ultimately anti-Roman policy. The incident of the soothsayer is probably imaginary but refers to an historical event

of 301 B.C., i.e., the salvation of Mithridatis II by his friend Dimi-
trios of Macedonia, who later became famous as "The Besieger"
(see "King Dimitrios").

DAYS OF 1909, '10, AND '11   p. 161

Printed December 6, 1928.
Loosely rhymed *abcde, ffffcfc,* and *gfhdhdf.*
See the note to "Days of 1903."

MYRIS: ALEXANDRIA, A.D. 340   p. 162

Printed April 19, 1929.
This is the longest of Cavafy's published poems. Of the surviving
unpublished poems, "King Claudius" is longer by twenty-one
lines.
The protagonist and scene are imaginary. The date places them
in a time of great political and religious upheaval: civil strife be-
tween the sons of Constantine the Great, and religious clashes be-
tween the supporters of Arios and Athanasios in Alexandria, result-
ing in the latter's banishment to Rome. For the Serapeion, see the
note to "Priest at the Serapeion."

ALEXANDER JANNAIOS AND ALEXANDRA   p. 165

Printed July 19, 1929.
Alexander Jannaios was the most famous and ruthless of the As-
monaean (see "Aristovoulos") kings of Judaea. He reigned from
103 to 76 B.C., during the eighty-year period of Jewish autonomy
which began in 142 with the revolt of the Asmonaeans (Maccabees)
against the Selefkids and their hellenizing influence. Alexandra-Sa-
lome, his wife, was the widow of his brother, Aristovoulos I (104-
103 B.C.), founder of the secular Asmonean dynasty, and the

mother of the prematurely murdered Aristovoulos III; she succeded Alexander from 76 to 69 B.C.

Judas Maccabaius, a priest of the Asmonaean clan, led, in 167 B.C, the popular rising of the Orthodox Jews against Antiochos IV Epiphanis (see ''To Antiochos Epiphanis'') and the hellenizing aristocracy of the Jewish clergy. After his death (160 B.C.), his four brothers (John, Simon, Eleazar, and Jonathan) continued the struggle with ever-increasing political emphasis, until they drove the Selefkid garrison out of Jerusalem (142 B.C.). Subsequently, the Asmoneans retained the religious and political power as a hereditary right but at the cost of dwindling popular support and of their cultural hellenization until Judaea was finally subjugated by Rome (37 B.C.).

LOVELY WHITE FLOWERS   p. 166

Printed October 3, 1929.

Each line really consists of two lines of either six or seven syllables, sporadically rhymed. In the Greek text of this poem, the effect, according to Seferis, is that of a popular song.

COME, O KING OF THE LACEDAIMONIANS   p. 167

Printed October 26, 1929.

This poem takes the events related in ''In Sparta'' one stage further. Kratisiklia was eventually executed by the successor to her son's Egyptian patron, Ptolemy IV. The quotation is from Plutarch's *Life of Kleomenis*, 28.

IN THE SAME SPACE   p. 168

Printed December 9, 1929.
Lines of 13-13, 15-14, and 15 syllables.

THE MIRROR IN THE FRONT HALL   p. 169

Printed February 3, 1930.
Sporadically rhymed. The metrical pattern of the last stanza is
12-12-10-12-12-12 syllables.

HE ASKED ABOUT THE QUALITY   p. 170

Printed May 15, 1930.
Sporadically rhymed.

TO HAVE TAKEN THE TROUBLE   p. 172

Printed July 8, 1930.
The anonymous protagonist is a fictional character placed by Ca-
vafy between 128 and 123 B.C. Kakergetis (= Malefactor) was the
nickname of Ptolemy VIII Evergetis (= Benefactor; see "Envoys
from Alexandria"), also dubbed Physkon (= Bladder), father of
Ptolemy IX Sotir, commonly known as Lathyros (= Chick-pea; see
"Those Who Fought for the Achaian League"). Zabinas (= Slave)
was the nickname of Alexander II, the alleged son of the adventurer
Alexander Valas (see "Of Dimitrios Sotir" and "The Favor of Al-
exander Valas"), who usurped the throne of Syria (128-123 B.C.)
with the help of Ptolemy VIII and was killed by Antiochos VIII
Grypos (= Hooknose). John Hyrkanos I, son of Simon Maccabaius
(see "Alexander Jannaios and Alexandra"), was king of Judaea
from 134 to 104 B.C., and naturally profited from the feuds raging
around the throne of Syria.

FOLLOWING THE RECIPE OF ANCIENT GRECO-SYRIAN
MAGICIANS   p. 174

Printed February 23, 1931.

266

IN THE YEAR 200 B.C.   p. 175

Probably first written June 1916, with the title "Except the La-
cedaimonians."
Printed September 10, 1931.
The title (cf. "In a Large Greek Colony, 200 B.C.") places the
poem at an optimum moment of the decline of Hellenism: some 130
years after Alexander's victories, and three years before the battle
of Cynoscephalae, where Philip V (see the note to "The Battle of
Magnesia"), the last of the Macedonian Philips, was crushingly de-
feated by the Romans. It is also ten years before the defeat of An-
tiochos III the Great at Magnesia (see the same note), which marked
the Roman conquest of "the great new Hellenic world" extolled in
the poem.
The opening line quotes from the dedicatory inscription which
Alexander the Great ordered to be engraved on the three hundred
Persian panoplies he sent to the Athenian Parthenon. Granikos, Is-
sus, and Arbela were the three battles (334, 333 and 331 B.C.) that
decided Alexander's Persian campaign.
Concerning the stubborn refusal of the Lacedaimonians (= Spar-
tans) to participate in that campaign, it is worth remembering that
they had lost, since 371 B.C., their military supremacy to the The-
bans, who were eventually crushed in 338 B.C. by the Macedonians.
Indeed, by the third century B.C., the fighting power of the Lace-
daimonians had dwindled to no more than seven hundred men, ow-
ing to the unwillingness of their kings to adapt their antiquated con-
stitution to the new historical and social circumstances (see note to
"In Sparta").
The "Common Greek Language" (or *Koine*), based on the Attic
dialect, became, for at least six hundred years, the international lan-
guage of both the East and Christendom. Bactria was a satrapy be-
tween northern Afghanistan and southern Uzbekistan; it remained
under Greek cultural influence until 140 B.C. In 1920, Cavafy wrote

a poem ("Coins") about the Greeks in Bactria, which remained unpublished until 1968.

DAYS OF 1908   p. 177

Probably first written July 1921, with the title "The Summer of 1895."
Printed November 17, 1932.
Loosely rhymed *aab, cdcee, fdbghci, djd, caa, cba,* and *klmnopq.*
See the note to "Days of 1903," but also that to "Days of 1901."

JULIAN AT THE MYSTERIES   p. 181

Written November 1896, and first entitled "Julian at Eleusis."
In eleven-syllable lines.
This is the earliest of Cavafy's extant poems concerning Julian the Apostate (see the note to "Julian Seeing Contempt"). Its source is almost certainly the following passage from Gibbon's *Decline and Fall* (Ch. XXIII):

His residence at Athens [c. 354] confirmed this unnatural alliance of philosophy and superstition. He obtained the privilege of a solemn initiation into the mysteries of Eleusis, which, amidst the general decay of the Grecian worship, still retained some vestiges of their primaeval sanctity. . . . As these ceremonies were performed in the depths of caverns, and in the silence of the night; and as the inviolable secret of the mysteries was preserved by the discretion of the initiated, I shall not presume to describe the horrid sounds, and fiery apparitions, which were presented to the senses, or the imagination, of the credulous aspirant.

Equally relevant is Gibbon's note at this point:

When Julian, in a momentary panic, made the sign of the cross, the daemons instantly disappeared (Greg. Naz. Orat. iii,

p. 71). Gregory supposes that they were frightened, but the priests declared that they were indignant.

The Bishop of Nicomedia mentioned in line 21 was Julian's spiritual tutor (see "Julian in Nicomedia").

KING CLAUDIUS   p. 183

Written July 1899.

In eleven-syllable lines. This is Cavafy's longest extant poem (see note to "Myris: Alexandria, A.D. 340").

Following an early attempt to translate *Much Ado About Nothing* (of which only a paraphrase of "Sigh no more, ladies . . ." has survived), Cavafy wrote at least four poems directly derived from Shakespeare: "Lights, Lights, Lights" (1893), "The State of Denmark" (1899), "King Claudius" (1899), "Antony's Ending" (1907). Although only the titles of the first two have survived, their reference to *Hamlet* (III, ii and I, iv) is indisputable. Cavafy's familiarity with Shakespeare's plays is also substantiated by two early essays (1891 and 1893), of which the first translates, and comments upon, passages from *Measure for Measure*, III, i.

WHEN THE WATCHMAN SAW THE LIGHT   p. 187

Written January 1900.

Lines 1-8, 11-12, and 23-25 have thirteen syllables; all the rest have twelve syllables; rhymed *aabbccddeeffgghhiijjkkk* (rhymes *e, i,* and *j* are almost identical).

Concerning the interchangeability of rulers, cf. "In a Township of Asia Minor."

The poem is directly derived from the prologue to Aeschylus' *Agamemnon*. Three months earlier, Cavafy had written a poem inspired by Aeschylus' *Persians* entitled "The Naval Battle," and this too remained unpublished until 1968. Aeschylus appears among the collected poems in the epigraph to "Unfaithfulness" and in "Young Men of Sidon." Among the rejected poems, "The Vote of Athena" (1894) is probably derived from Aeschylus' *Eumenides*.

GROWING IN SPIRIT   p. 188

Written probably June 1903.

The metrical pattern is 13-12-13-13-13-12-12-13-12-13 syllables, rhymed *abcddbecea* (rhymes *b* and *e* are almost identical).

The title of the original literally means "Invigoration."

SEPTEMBER, 1903   p. 189

According to a note by Cavafy, this poem and the one that follows it "were really written in October and December 1903 [respectively], but were perfected and catalogued in January 1904." For the poet's further comment on these two poems, see *Passions and Ancient Days*, p. 63. See also the note to "Days of 1903."

The metrical pattern is 13-11, 12-12-11-12-12, and 11-12-13-11 syllables.

DECEMBER, 1903   p. 190

See the note to the previous poem and to "Days of 1903."

ON THE STAIRS   p. 191

Written February 1904.

AT THE THEATRE   p. 192

Written March 1904.

POSEIDONIANS p. 193

Written August 1906.
The epigraph contains a number of omissions and alterations.
Poseidonia, near the modern town of Salerno, is better known
under its Roman name, Paestum. As a Greek colony, it was
founded around 600 B.C. and flourished until 438 B.C. The custom
mentioned by Athenaeus probably dates from the end of the fourth
century B.C. Around 390 B.C., Poseidonia was captured by the Lu-
cani and held by them until 273 B.C., when it became a Latin colony
and its name was changed.

ANTONY'S ENDING p. 194

Written June 1907.
This is the earliest of Cavafy's poems concerning Mark Antony
and the year 31 B.C. (see "The God Abandons Antony," "Alex-
andrian Kings," "Kaisarion," "In Alexandria, 31 B.C.," and "In
a Township of Asia Minor"). It is directly derived from Shake-
speare's *Antony and Cleopatra*, IV, xv (see note to "King Clau-
dius").

HIDDEN THINGS p. 195

Written June 1911.

ON HEARING OF LOVE p. 196

Written June 1911.
Rhymed *abcacb*.

"THE REST I WILL TELL TO THOSE DOWN IN HADES" p. 197

First written November 1893.
Rewritten February 1913.

Rhymed *aabccdded* and *be*.

The title is a quotation from Sophocles' *Ajax* 865, i.e., Ajax's last words before his suicide. The scene and the anonymous protagonists are imaginary.

THE PHOTOGRAPH   p. 198

Written April 1913.

The title of the original means "So" or "Thus."

GOING BACK HOME FROM GREECE   p. 199

Written July 1914.

The scene and the anonymous speaker are fictitious. His interlocutor, Hermippos, could be either the third century B.C. biographer or the grammarian of the time of Trajan and Hadrian (A.D. 98-138).

EXILES   p. 200

Written October 1914.

Rhymed *ababcdcdefefghghijijklkl* (rhymes *d* and *g* are almost identical, and rhymes *f* and *i* consonant).

The anonymous exiles of the poem cannot be identified precisely, yet their situation falls well within what Cavafy called "historical possibility." The scene is set in Alexandria, obviously after its conquest by the Arabs (641) and probably soon after the murder of the Byzantine emperor Michael III (see "Imenos") by his co-emperor Basil I (867-886), founder of the Macedonian dynasty. The mention of Christians who "seem to lean toward Rome" further points to the period of the Photian schism (867-870) when its initiator, the Patriarch of Constantinople, Photios, had been deposed by the emperor, and most of his friends had been driven into exile. The "Panopolitan" of line 17 is the Egyptian-Greek poet Nonnos (fifth c. A.D.), mentioned by name in line 15.

THEOPHILOS PALAIOLOGOS   p. 201

The date of the first version, now lost, is not known; in March 1903 Cavafy rewrote a poem entitled "I would rather die than live" (a quotation from Frantzis' *Chronicle*, III, 7). The extant version is undated but certainly later. Since the manuscript is accompanied by relevant quotations from, and references to, books published in 1909 and 1914, I have tentatively dated the poem to the latter year.

Theophilos Palaiologos was a kinsman of Constantine XI Palaiologos, the last emperor of Byzantium. Grammarian, humanist, and mathematician, he was given command of the troops defending the sector of the Gate of Silyvria during the siege of Constantinople by the Turks in 1453, and was killed during the final battle, fighting at the side of the emperor.

In 1921 Cavafy wrote another poem on the fall of Constantinople, "Parthen," which also remained unpublished until 1968.

AND I LOUNGED AND LAY ON THEIR BEDS   p. 202

Written September 1915.

HALF AN HOUR   p. 203

Written January 1917.

SIMEON   p. 204

Written July 1917.

The anonymous speaker and his listener, Mevis (cf. "Sophist Leaving Syria"), are both fictitious characters. Cavafy places them in Syria c. A.D. 454, i.e., thirty-five years after Simeon Stylites the Elder had ascended his pillar and five years before his death. By that time, this first Stylite had "acquired considerable fame and was visited by people of many nations: Ishmaelites, Persians, Armenians, Iberians, Spaniards, British, etc.'' (*The Oxford Dictionary of Byzantium*).

The other historical characters mentioned are Libanius (314-c.393), the Syrian rhetorician who taught Julian and St. John Chrysostom ''an atticizing Greek, which is always the result of painstaking labor, and often tortuous and difficult'' (*The Oxford Classical Dictionary*), and Meleager (fl. 100 B.C.), the Syrian poet and philosopher whose epigrams ''infuse erotic feeling into the traditional forms of epitaph and dedication, combining remarkable technical adroitness with apparently genuine emotion'' (*ibid.*).

The poet Lamon, who serves as a pretext for this dramatic monologue, is also a fictitious character. In choosing his name, Cavafy may have had in mind the ancient scholarly joke: ''In the lands of the blind, Lamon [= the one-eyed man] reigns.''

Cavafy's early preoccupation with Simeon as an important poetic theme can be discerned from an English note in his hand, written c. 1899 and inserted into his copy of Gibbon (Ch. XXXVII):

This great, this wonderful saint is surely an object to be singled out in ecclesiastical history for admiration and study. He has been, perhaps, the only man who has dared to be really *alone* . . . I have met with only one poem on Simeon Stylites [i.e., Tennyson's ''Stylites''], but it is in no way worthy of the subject . . . Its great defect lies in its form of a monologue . . . It was a very difficult task—a task reserved, perhaps, for some mighty king of art—to find fitting language for so great a saint, so wonderful a man.

For the full text of the note, see *Passions* and *Ancient Days*, pp. 67-68.

THE BANDAGED SHOULDER   p. 205

Written May 1919.

ON THE OUTSKIRTS OF ANTIOCH   p. 206

Almost certainly written between November 1932 and April 1933. Although prepared for the printer by Cavafy, this poem appeared for the first time in the posthumous edition of 1935 (see editor's introduction) and has been included ever since in the *corpus* of the "Published Poems."

Vavylas—better known as St. Babylas—bishop of Antioch (c. 237-250) and martyr, had been reburied in the precinct of the temple and oracle of Apollo, in the grove of Daphni (a suburb of Antioch), at the initiative of Julian's half-brother Gallus (see "Julian in Nicomedia"). The priests of Apollo abandoned the temple, which they considered to have been polluted by this burial, and the Christians built a church over Vavylas' tomb. When Julian arrived in Antioch (July 362; see the notes to "Julian Seeing Contempt" and "Julian and the Antiochians"), he gave orders for the church to be demolished, for Vavylas' bones to be carried back to their original grave, and for the ritual purification of the place. On October 22, 362, the roof of the temple and the internationally famous statue of Apollo were destroyed by a fire which was attributed to the vengeance of the Christians.

BIOGRAPHICAL NOTE

CONSTANTINE P. CAVAFY (Kavafis), born in Alexandria, Egypt, in 1863, was the ninth and last child of Constantinopolitan parents. His father, Peter Cavafy, left Constantinople as a young man (in 1836) to join his elder brother George in England, where the two worked with Greek business firms in Manchester, London, and Liverpool. They returned to London in 1846, and three years later founded Cavafy Brothers, an export-import firm that prospered for some years dealing in Egyptian cotton and Manchester textiles. In 1894 Peter revisited Constantinople and there married Hariklia, daughter of a diamond merchant, George Photiadis, of Yeniköy on the Bosphorus (she was then a girl of fourteen). He left her in his mother's house in Pera and returned the following year to bring her and her firstborn son to England. In August of that year (1850) he obtained British nationality, and he and his family spent the next few years in Liverpool. In late 1854 or early 1855 the family moved to Alexandria, and the Alexandrian branch of Cavafy Brothers soon became the central office of the family firm. Peter died in 1870, leaving the family poorly provided for. Hariklia and her seven sons moved to England two years later. The eldest son, George, became manager of the family firm in London, and the second son, Peter, manager in Liverpool. Their inexperience caused the ruin of the family fortunes. George's injudiciousness largely contributed to the liquidation of the firm in 1879, and Peter managed to lose their private inheritance by unwise speculations. With the exception of George, who stayed on in London, the family returned to a life of genteel poverty in Alexandria.

The seven years that Cavafy spent in England, between the ages of nine and sixteen, were important in the shaping of his poetic sensibility. Apart from his reading in English literature, he became so much at home in the English language and so familiar with English manners that the influence of both remained with him throughout his life (he is reported to have spoken his native Greek with a slight British accent until the day he died). His first verse was written in English (signed "Constantine Cavafy"), and both his subsequent practice as a poet and his limited prose criticism demonstrate a substantial familiarity with the English poetic tradition, in particular the work of Shakespeare, Browning, and Oscar Wilde.

Immediately after Cavafy returned to Alexandria from London, he enrolled for a brief period at the Hermis Lyceum, a commercial school that served the leading families in the Greek community. This is the only instance of formal education indicated by the biographical data currently available to us. During the same period he began a historical dictionary that was interrupted, significantly, at the entry "Alexander." Then, in 1882, before the British bombardment of Alexandria, Hariklia again moved her family abroad for a three-year interval, this time back to Constantinople, where her father gave them room in his house at Yeniköy and where she and the three sons with her (including Constantine) lived on what her other three sons, who had returned to Alexandria, were able to send her from their scanty earnings. It was a time of poverty and discomfort, but it proved to be another significant stage in the development of Cavafy's sensibility. He wrote his first poems—in English, French, and Greek—during this interval, and he apparently had his first homosexual affairs.

There is also some evidence that he began to think of a career in politics or journalism, but was discouraged because he had never attended law school. In any case, soon after his return to Alexandria in 1885, he received a press card as correspondent for the Alexandrian newspaper *Telegraphos*, and by 1888 he was working at the Egyptian Stock Exchange as assistant to his brother Aristidis. But much of his ambition during these years was devoted to the writing of poems and a few prose essays, including one in English entitled "Give Back the Elgin Marbles."

At the age of twenty-nine Cavafy took up an appointment as special clerk in the Irrigation Service (Third Circle) of the Ministry of Public Works, where he had apparently been doing piece-work as an unsalaried clerk for as long as three years, while waiting for an appropriate vacancy to occur. He held this appointment for the next thirty years, and it provided the principal source of his income, supplemented by speculative earnings (sometimes quite substantial) on the Egyptian Stock Exchange, which admitted him as a broker in 1894. His Greek citizenship precluded his becoming a member of the so-called "permanent staff" of the Service, which was restricted to British or Egyptian subjects, but during the course of his career he received regular increases in salary (from £7 a month in 1892 to £33 a month in 1919), and he retired in 1922 with the rank of "Assistant Director." He continued to live in Alexandria until his death, from cancer of the larynx, in 1933. It is recorded that he received the holy communion of the Orthodox Church shortly before dying, and that his last motion was to draw a circle on a blank sheet of paper and then place a period in the middle of the circle.

From the outline of this sparse history, it would seem that Cavafy's richest life had to be the inner life sustained by his personal relations and his artistic creativity. Yet what little is known of the poet's social life suggests an image that is equally undramatic. There is now some reason to question the traditional view of Cavafy as an isolated figure hiding behind the dim candlelight of a stuffy, booklined room (Sareyiannis' memoir indicates that the poet received visitors often and was known to be a stimulating, loquacious host when the mood struck him). At the same time, the bare facts of his biography suggest an unusually restricted circle of personal relations. He lived with his mother until her death in 1899, then with his unmarried brothers, and for most of his mature years, alone. The poet himself identified only two love affairs, both apparently transitory (see the comment on ''September, 1903'' and ''December, 1903'' in *C. P. Cavafy: Passions and Ancient Days*, New York, 1971, p. 63). A number of personal notes—largely unpublished—reveal that Cavafy was tormented until his middle forties not by complications resulting from homosexual relationships (as a number of his erotic poems might lead one to think) but by guilt over what he felt to be a relentless autoeroticism. His one intimate, long-standing friendship, so far as is known, was with Alexander Singopoulos, whom Cavafy designated his heir and literary executor some ten years before his death, that is, when the poet was sixty years old.

Cavafy did maintain several influential literary relationships during his later years, including a twenty-year acquaintance with E. M. Forster; and as his unique contribution to twentieth-century poetry began to receive some local recognition, he became one of the few literary personalities European visitors to Alexandria might try to approach. Several of those who managed to search him out have reported that Cavafy was not only a receptive host but a learned conversationalist who had the fascinating capacity to gossip about historical figures from the distant past so as to make them seem a part of some scandalous intrigue taking place in the Alexandrian world immediately below the poet's second-floor balcony. Yet for all his local renown, Cavafy remained virtually unrecognized in Greece until late in his career (an article on his poetry by Grigori Xenopoulos in 1903 is a revealing exception), and his own attitude toward the public presentation of his work suggested an "uncommon esthetic asceticism" (as expressed in the introduction to *Passions and Ancient Days*). Cavafy never offered a volume of his poems for sale during his lifetime; his method of distributing his work was to give friends and relatives the several pamphlets of his poems that he had printed privately and a folder of his latest broadsheets or offprints held together by a large clip. The only evidence of some public recognition in Greece during his later years was his receipt, in 1926, of the Order of the Phoenix from the Greek dictator Pangalos, and his appointment, in 1930, to the International Committee for the Rupert Brooke memorial statue that was placed on the island of Skyros. The latter may have been partly a consequence of the recognition Cavafy had gained in England by that time, including publication of "Ithaka" in T. S. Eliot's *Criterion* and the enthusiastic interest of T. E. Lawrence, Arnold Toynbee, anad others who had been introduced to his work by E. M. Forster.

Though Cavafy met various men of letters during his several trips to Athens (including a four-month visit for medical reasons shortly before his death), he did not receive his full measure of appreciation from the Athenian literati until some time after the publication of his first collected edition in 1935. It seems likely that his importance went relatively unrecognized before his death for exactly those reasons that have now established him as perhaps the most original and influential Greek poet of this century: his uncompromising distaste, in his mature years, for rhetoric of the kind then prevalent among his contemporary poets in mainland Greece; his almost prosaic frugality in the use of figures and metaphors; his constant evocation of spoken rhythms and colloquialisms; his frank, avant-garde treatment of homosexual themes; his reintroduction of epigrammatic and dramatic modes that had remained largely dormant since Hellenistic times; his often esoteric but brilliantly alive sense of history; his commitment to Hellenism, coupled with an astute cynicism about politics; his aesthetic perfectionism; his creation of a rich mythic world during his mature years. These attributes, not yet in fashion during his day, and his refusal to enter the marketplace even to buy prestige, may have prevented him from realizing all but the most private rewards of his genius. They are also among the characteristics likely to assure him an enduring place not only in the Greek tradition but in world literature more generally.

E.K.[1]

[1] The biographical details in this Note are based in large part on data generously supplied by Stratis Tsirkas and by Robert Liddell. Mr. Liddell is the author of *Cavafy: A Critical Biography* (London: Duckworth, 1974; New York: Pocket Books, 1978).

ALPHABETICAL INDEX OF TITLES

The Lockert Library of Poetry in Translation

George Seferis: Collected Poems (1924-1955), translated, edited, and introduced by Edmund Keeley and Philip Sherrard

Collected Poems of Lucio Piccolo, translated and edited by Brian Swann and Ruth Feldman

C. P. Cavafy: Collected Poems, translated by Edmund Keeley and Philip Sherrard and edited by George Savadis

Benny Anderson: Selected Poems, translated by Alexander Taylor

Selected Poetry of Andrea Zanzotto, translated and edited by Ruth Feldman and Brian Swann

Poems of René Char, translated by Mary Ann Caws and Jonathan Griffin

"The Survivor" and Other Poems by Tadeusz Różewicz, translated and introduced by Magnus J. Krynski and Robert A. Maguire

"Harsh World" and Other Poems by Ángel González, translated by Donald D. Walsh

Dante's "Rime," translated by Patrick S. Diehl

Selected Later Poems of Marie Luise Kaschnitz, translated by Lisel Mueller

The Dawn Is Always New: Selected Poetry of Rocco Scotellaro, translated by Ruth Feldman and Brian Swann

Sounds, Feelings, Thoughts: Seventy Poems by Wisława Szymborska, translated and introduced by Magnus J. Krynski and Robert A. Maguire

The Man I Pretend to Be: "The Colloquies" and Selected Poems of Guido Gozzano, translated and edited by Michael Palma, with an introductory essay by Eugenio Montale

D'Après Tout: Poems by Jean Follain, translated by Heather McHugh

Song of Something Else: Selected Poems of Gunnar Ekelöf, translated by Leonard Nathan and James Larson

The Ellipse: Selected Poems of Leonardo Sinisgalli, translated by W. S. DiPiero